Vol. XXIII., No. 1.   1897.   Whole No. 81.

PROCEEDINGS

OF THE

UNITED STATES

NAVAL INSTITUTE.

VOLUME XXIII.

EDITED BY H. G. DRESEL.

PUBLISHED QUARTERLY BY THE INSTITUTE.

ANNAPOLIS, MD.

PRESS OF THE FRIEDENWALD CO.
BALTIMORE, MD.

The writers are responsible only for the contents of their respective articles.

CONTENTS.

NOTICE.

ANNAPOLIS, MD., *February 10, 1897.*

Having carefully read the four essays submitted in competition for the prize offered by the U. S. Naval Institute for the year 1897, we have the honor to announce that, in accordance with Article XI. of the Constitution, the prize is awarded to the essay bearing the motto, " Everything in order," on Torpedo-Boat Policy, by Lieutenant R. C. Smith, U. S. Navy.

Honorable mention is accorded in the order named to the essays bearing the mottoes: (1) " From little spark may burst a mighty flame," on A Proposed Uniform Course of Instruction for the Naval Militia, by Mr. H. G. Dohrman, Associate Member, U. S. Naval Institute; (2) " And another came, saying, Lord, behold, here is Thy pound, which I have kept laid up in a napkin; for I feared Thee, because Thou art an austere man," on Torpedoes in Exercise and Battle, by Lieutenant John M. Ellicott, U. S. Navy.

EDWIN WHITE, Commander, U. S. Navy.
ASA WALKER, Commander, U. S. Navy.
B. F. TILLEY, Commander, U. S. Navy.
E. B. UNDERWOOD, Lieutenant, U. S. Navy.
DAVID DANIELS, Lieutenant, U. S. Navy.
N. M. TERRY, A. M., Ph. D.,
Professor, U. S. Naval Academy.
H. G. DRESEL, Lieutenant, U. S. Navy.
Members, Board of Control.

NOTICE.

Further discussions on articles in this number are requested. They will be published in succeeding numbers.

H. G. DRESEL, Secretary and Treasurer.

THE PROCEEDINGS

UNITED STATES NAVAL INSTITUTE.

Vol. XXIII., No. 1. **1897.** **Whole No. 81.**

PRIZE ESSAY, 1897.

MOTTO: " Everything in Order."

[COPYRIGHTED.]

TORPEDO-BOAT POLICY.

BY LIEUTENANT R. C. SMITH, U. S. Navy.

INTRODUCTORY.

It seems probable that the United States, after many years
hesitation, is now about to enter on a policy of torpedo-boat
construction. The desirableness of such action is hardly open
to criticism.

We shall have twenty-three boats of the different classes when
all that are now authorized shall have been accepted. An inspec-
tion of the lists of foreign warships will show that the ratio of
torpedo-boats to other classes is nearly as two to one. Our
ratio at present is more nearly the reciprocal of this.

It cannot of course be assumed that in every country there is
the same ratio to be observed between the various elements of
the fleet. The numbers of torpedo-boats, for instance, will be
influenced by the general policy and the extent and character of
the coast, as well as by the actual size of the navy. It is not
intended here to take up more than casually the question of
the number of boats it would be desirable to build in the United

States, but it may be remarked in this connection that whatever arguments have been advanced in other countries in favor of torpedo-boats, either in reference to their use with the squadron as circumstances indicated, or to the special features of the coast which might lend themselves to torpedo-boat operations, apply with if anything greater force to the case of the United States.

It has been held abroad that torpedo-boats are the weapon of the weaker naval power. A power that is strong in ships will be able to bring commanding numbers against the ships of a weaker enemy. She has no imperative need for many torpedo-boats. On the other hand, the weaker power here finds its opportunity. The latter requires torpedo-boats, the former torpedo-boat destroyers. Continuing the argument, a nation which may be attacked by superior numbers on its own coast may find the torpedo-boat a weapon of the greatest value.

But it is when the natural features of our coast are considered that the argument in favor of torpedo-boats presents itself in the strongest light. The extent and configuration of the coast, and especially the amount of inland-water navigation, seem to make the torpedo-boat a weapon peculiarly suited to our special requirements.

Thus there cannot be any reasonable doubt as to the desirableness of increasing materially the torpedo-flotilla; but there may be, and in all probability is, considerable doubt as to the characteristics of its components. In the past twenty years there have been first and second-class torpedo-boats, sea-going torpedo-boats, torpedo-cruisers, torpedo-rams, torpedo-gunboats or catchers, torpedo-vedette-boats, torpedo-boat destroyers. Which of these different types should we copy after for the present, and what should be the military features of the types selected? As we have little experience of our own, the practice of other nations will be for the present a useful guide.

It is necessary here to review, in a general way, the course of torpedo-boat construction abroad, after which we shall be in a better position to form an opinion as to our own needs.

The vessels to be considered are those in which the automobile torpedo forms the chief or a very important feature of the armament. Submarine torpedo-boats are not here included. The subject is a large one in itself, and requires separate treatment.

TORPEDO-BOATS PROPER.

...pedo-boat, from all accounts, owes its origin ...ches fitted for spar-torpedoes, built first by Thorny... ...rrow and the Herreshoffs. When machine and rapid-fire guns practically put an end to this form of weapon, it was a step only to the automobile torpedo in the same type of boat.

A precursor of the spar-torpedo launch was the Miranda, a fast river-launch, built by Thornycroft in 1871. She was just short of 50 feet in length, and made 16¼ knots, at that time an unprecedented speed. The hull was of Bessemer steel. She had two cockpits and a low glass deck-house. A locomotive boiler supplied steam at 120 pounds pressure to a two-cylinder vertical engine. Here were many features of later torpedo-boats.

In 1873 Thornycroft turned out a torpedo-launch for Norway, which I believe was called the Rasp, and which was a great advance on any previous attempt. This boat was 57 feet long and made 17¼ knots on trial. She had compound engines and the usual locomotive boiler. She was fitted to tow a torpedo from the top of the smoke-pipe. The Glimt for Sweden in 1875 was very similar and made 18 knots.

The Herreshoffs were among the earliest in this field. Their Lightning was built for the Bureau of Ordnance in 1876. She was a wooden launch of 58 feet over all and weighed about three tons. The boiler was of the patent safety-coil type, supplying steam at 140 pounds pressure to a two-cylinder 5 by 10 engine running at 400 revolutions a minute. This boat actually made in 60 minutes on trial 20.3 statute miles with and against the tide, equivalent to 17.6 knots. She was fitted for the spar-torpedo.

A noted boat of this time (1876) was the Gitana, a yacht built by Thornycroft for the Baroness Rothschild to run on Lake Geneva. She was of steel plates, 86 feet long on the water, and displaced 29 tons. A locomotive boiler supplied steam at 100 pounds pressure to a three-cylinder compound engine running at 325 revolutions. She was guaranteed to make 36 miles in 2 hours, but actually made 43 miles in 1 hour and 48 minutes, or at the rate of 20¾ knots.

Thornycroft's Lightning for the British government dated from 1877. She was 84 feet long and was designed for 18 knots, but made 19.4 on preliminary trials. This was the first real torpedo-boat. Her armament was the Whitehead torpedo discharged from the forward deck. She was made rather heavier and with fuller lines than her predecessors, in order to withstand rough weather if necessary. She also had more complete cabin arrangements to permit remaining at sea for longer intervals. Her engines made 350 revolutions with 120 pounds of steam. In other respects she resembled earlier boats.

Messrs. Yarrow & Co., of Poplar, had also turned out a number of fast launches of various sizes. Their first torpedo-boat was built for the Argentine in 1874. She was of steel, 55 feet long and made 12½ knots on 65 indicated horse-power. She was fitted for the McEvoy spar-torpedo.

In 1877 they built Nos. 17 and 18 for the English government. These boats were 86 feet long, of 33 tons displacement and made 21 knots on 450 indicated horse-power. Their armament was two torpedo-tubes. No. 14, by the same firm the following year, was practically the same size, but made 21.94 knots on 550 horse-power, and was the fastest vessel of its day.

Boats now began to be known as first and second-class, according as they were of a size to act independently or were designed to be carried on shipboard. The distinction still holds generally, though boats for ships are sometimes now called third-class.

The second-class boats were first fitted with side frames for discharging the 14-inch torpedo. The torpedo was lowered over the side and was started parallel to the keel-line by its own motive power, using a laniard to haul back the starting lever. The speed of the boat required to be reduced to permit this.

Steam was next used for the discharge. The torpedoes were laid in troughs on the forecastle and ejected by a steam piston with a stroke of 7 feet. This method did not require the speed of the boat to be slackened. It was designed by Yarrow.

Air-discharge was the next form, and this was used mostly in the larger boats, until followed much later (about 1884) by the now almost universal gunpowder method.

In 1878 there were several French boats, built by various firms, of 108 feet and 45 tons. Their speed was 19 knots. They had two torpedo-tubes.

The Herreshoffs built a boat for the English government in 1879. She was fitted with one of their coil boilers. The first apparent effect on English practice was the fitting of second-class boats to take live steam from the ship's boilers through a flexible pipe, in order to hasten the time of getting underway. Thornycroft's tubulous boiler followed about four years later, the first of which went into a Missionary steamer on the Congo. The Herreshoff boat was about 60 feet long and realized 16 knots. There were several novelties besides the coil boiler. She was of composite structure with steel frames, planked below the water and plated above. The shaft inclined downward at first, but was brought back to the horizontal by running it through a curved brass tube which gave it a long bearing. The shaft had sufficient elasticity to revolve in this position. The screw was well under the body of the boat. The long bearing formed a sort of fin-keel, as well as a surface condenser for the exhaust steam. As the deadwood was cut away abaft the screw, it also formed a pivot for turning and made the boat very handy.

In 1880 Thornycroft had reached a type of first-class boat for England, 90 feet long with a speed of 22 knots. This boat was fitted with a ram bow as a result of an experience in a collision at Portsmouth in February, 1880, in which a boat with a straight stem had her bow completely stove in against the side of another boat. Apropos of this, Mr. Donaldson, of the Thornycroft firm, said in a lecture before the Royal United Service Institution in April, 1881, "All our boats are now fitted with the ram bow, strengthened so as to be useful as a means of offense in an action between boats." This principle seems to me a very important one and will be referred to again.

The armament of this boat was three Whitehead torpedoes, two in transporting carriages, one on each side of the deck, and the third in a tube on the bow. The tube was pivoted, permitting it to be trained ahead and on either beam. The torpedo was ejected by a telescopic impulse tube actuated by compressed air.

The Batoum was built by Yarrow for Russia in 1880. She was 100 feet long and made 22 knots. She was the first so-called sea-going torpedo-boat, and made the trip from London to Nikolaief, 4800 miles, at an average speed of 11 knots. She was fitted with twin bow tubes and carried four 19-foot Whiteheads. This was the first boat to be fitted with a turtle-back deck.

In 1881 Thornycroft built a boat for Denmark, the Svaerdfisken, of 110 feet, with twin bow tubes and an armament of four 19-foot, 15-inch Whiteheads. The discharge was by compressed air admitted in the tube behind the torpedo, which is the present method with air-discharge. Her torpedoes carried a charge of 80 pounds of gun-cotton and had a speed of 20 knots for 1000 yards. This boat was guaranteed to make 18 knots for 3 hours, but was expected to exceed that speed. She actually made 20.

In 1882 Yarrow completed a 100-foot boat for Italy of the Batoum type which made 22½ knots on trial. This was the highest record to date. This was considered to be a very efficient sea-going type. Ten similar boats had been navigated to the Mediterranean the previous year, and two across the Atlantic. This boat had all the Yarrow special features, such as bow and stern rudders, turtle-back deck and water-tight ash-pan. The bow rudder had been first used in 1878. It was arranged to raise and lower, or to drop altogether if it became entangled. Used in conjunction with the after one, it reduced the diameter of the turning circle practically one-half. The turtle-back deck has since become very common. It sheds the seas well, but a greater advantage is the added strength it gives to light structures by its curved surface. The water-tight ash-pan was an arrangement to prevent extinguishment of the fires in case the compartment was flooded.

Schichau, of Elbing, had also built torpedo-boats. In 1882 this firm built two boats for Italy of 100 feet and 40 tons, with a speed of 22 knots. The armament was two torpedo-tubes and a revolving-cannon.

The torpedo-boat had grown precariously to this stage in its existence. It had had its ups and downs, but through the exertions of builders and of officers who had faith in its mission, it had continued to develop.

It started off very well about the time the automobile began to displace the spar torpedo, and it was no longer necessary for the attacking boat actually to reach the side of the enemy. A very ordinary automobile torpedo had evidently many advantages over the spar-torpedo. But the revolving-cannon and the rapid-fire gun made their appearance, and in the then development of both torpedo and launch, the balance between attack and defense was, if anything, more than restored. The search-light and the defense-net capped the climax in favor of the defense.

But the torpedo continued to improve in speed and range and the torpedo-boat in size and speed. In fleet exercises and drills the boats occasionally scored successes, notwithstanding the search-lights, rapid-fire guns and defense-nets. We have followed the progress of the boat; the torpedo had kept pace with it. From a speed of 6 knots in 1867, it had increased to 20 knots in 1876, and to 24 knots in 1882. The range had also increased with the speed.

The torpedo-officers remained unshaken, enthusiasts they were called by their opponents, but it is worth noticing, however, that the enthusiasm came from a practical knowledge of the weapon, and represented the balance to the good after discounting uncertainties and failures.

But the boats were again to fall into disfavor. They were still small compared with those of to-day. Their endurance in coal, water, and provisions was limited; they were barely seaworthy; and, through buffeting, their crews were rapidly exhausted when cruising continuously in all weathers. Then, with their light and fast-moving machinery, breakdowns were numerous. The boats were sources of anxiety to the Admirals in command, and frequently had to be sent to port under convoy.

From now on, through this part of the subject, an attempt will be made to indicate the trend of opinion by a selection of quotations coincidently with a brief enumeration of the various types of boats as they appeared.

The firm of Normand & Co., of Havre, had built some of the French boats of 1878. In 1883 they built the Poti for Russia. She was 125 feet long and displaced 72 tons. She made 18½ knots on 570 horse-power. Her armament was two tubes and two revolving-cannon.

Between 1883 and 1890 the Elbing firm built sixty-three boats for Germany, now on the navy list, of from 121 to 128 feet, and 85 to 88 tons. On 1000 indicated horse-power they made from 19 to 22 knots. Their armament is two torpedo-tubes and two revolving-cannon.

Mr. J. S. White, of East Cowes, was the originator of the turnabout system of boats. By cutting away the deadwood aft and sometimes fitting a second rudder under the bow, he increased the manœuvering power considerably. One of the best known of his boats was the Swift for the English government in 1885.

She was 150 feet long and displaced 125 tons, quite a large boat for her day. She was sometimes referred to as a torpedo-catcher. Her trial speed was 20.8 knots. She had a three-cylinder compound engine and two locomotive boilers. The armament was two torpedo-tubes and six 3-pounders.

The Adler and Falke, by Yarrow for Austria in 1885, were the fastest boats to date. They were of 135 feet and 95 tons and made 22.4 knots on 1250 horse-power. This speed was probably exceeded at times, for Yarrow's boat for Italy in 1882 was credited with 22½ knots. The armament of the Adler and Falke was two bow tubes and two Nordenfelt guns. *Engineering,* January, 1886, page 14, has the following: "The bow of these boats is specially strong, the maximum weight of metal being put forward so as to stiffen the boat for ramming."

In this year and the next (1885-6) Thornycroft, White and Yarrow built fifty or sixty boats for England, varying from 113 to 128 feet, and from 60 to 75 tons. Their maximum speed was 22 knots. They carried two 3-pounders and from one to five torpedo-tubes. Lord Brassey states in the Annual for 1886, page 83, that these boats, which were laid down at the time of the Russian war-scare, were intended for use in the Baltic. It was expected that the Russian ships would be found locked up in port where torpedo-boats could not get at them, but that the English ships would be subject to attacks by the Russian boats. Hence these boats would probably have gone out with gun armaments alone, to act as a protection to the fleet against the Russian torpedo-boats. This idea anticipated by several years the modern torpedo-boat destroyers, which are really large and fast torpedo-boats with a heavy gun armament.

A suggestion to the same effect, but of a much earlier date, was made in a letter to the London *Engineer,* April, 1878, page 296, signed "Engineer." It was there advocated that each battleship should be protected from torpedo-boats by a small fast vessel of not less than 20 knots speed, with a sharp bow strengthened for ramming, and mounting a single bow-chaser. This vessel was to circle around the battleship at a distance of 500 yards and run down or destroy by gun-fire any hostile boat that might be encountered.

The following is the decision of the British Admiralty Board in regard to torpedo-boats, after the manœuvres of 1886, as quoted in Brassey, 1887, page 514:

"The practical tests during recent evolutions imposed upon first-class torpedo-boats, that is, boats intended for open sea service, and upwards of 100 feet in length, have shown that they could not, in actual warfare, stand the strain of the daily wear and tear to which they might be exposed. The discomfort and hardships which their crews have to endure in rough weather, the loss of speed to which, after steaming a certain number of hours at full pressure, they are subject, owing to the tendency of their necessarily contracted boiler tubes to choke, disqualify boats of these dimensions from taking the prominent part in warfare in the open seas which their adherents claim for them. The Board have therefore decided in future to build for sea-going purposes vessels of larger dimensions, capable of acting both on the offensive and defensive in torpedo-warfare, in the open sea. These vessels to be of the Rattlesnake type, capable of maintaining for many hours the initial speed of the ordinary torpedo-boat, armed with quick-firing guns, and another gun of a larger calibre, and affording adequate accommodations and protection to the complement they carry for sea-going purposes.

"The Board have decided upon adopting a new type of second-class torpedo-boat, capable of being lifted on board ships of a certain displacement, and which would be carried by the ship for service in the place of the larger or first-class torpedo-boats which are now supposed to accompany a squadron.

"The 125-foot torpedo-boats now building or built have, in most instances, been allotted to the defense of the great military ports and coaling stations, where they will remain."

We see here the line of argument that led to the torpedo-gun-boat or torpedo-boat catcher. The decision in regard to the 125-foot boats is scarcely open to criticism. Boats of that size must necessarily operate from a near-by base, which they can seek for shelter from the weather, or when pursued by the enemy, or to complete stores.

The decision as to second-class boats was apparently a retro-gression. The weight of opinion then and now was opposed to them, and for reasons which were well stated the previous year by *Engineering* (December, 1885, page 616):

"It would seem as if second-class torpedo-boats have become a thing of the past, so far, at least, as building any fresh ones is concerned. It is a question whether so small a class as a 60-

foot boat could ever be used effectively against an enemy excepting under the most favorable conditions. In addition to
this the second-class boats are useless for any general purposes
in times of peace, and occupy a vast deal of space on board the
vessels that carry them. The great improvements in speed made
lately by the larger navy pinnaces have made the second-class
boats less necessary, as the pinnaces carry torpedoes and are
a far handier and more seaworthy style of craft; useful also for
general purposes as a ship's steam launch."

The French at this time (1886) were building the Balny class,
so-called sea-going torpedo-boats (*torpilleurs de haute mer*) of 135
feet and 70 tons, armed with twin bow tubes and two revolving-
cannon. They were designed for 22 knots.

A since celebrated boat of that day (1886) was the Kotaka by
Yarrow for Japan. She was 170 feet long and displaced 190
tons. With 1400 indicated horse-power she made 19 knots.
She carried six torpedo-tubes and four machine guns. This
boat is one of the largest of the torpedo-boats proper, and in
size could be classed as a destroyer. She is very completely
subdivided and is protected by 1-inch plates over the machinery
space. In company with other boats, she was under the fire of
the forts in the attack on Port Arthur and suffered less than any.

In 1886 Messrs. J. & G. Thomson, of Clydebank, Glasgow,
built the Wiborg for Russia, of 142 feet and 142 tons, armed with
twin bow tubes and a training tube on deck for 19-foot torpedoes, and two revolving-cannon. Her speed on trial was 20.6
knots. This vessel embraced a number of novel features, among
them ¼-inch plating on the bow, and an inner skin in wake of
the water-line forward, with cellular spaces to be filled with an
obturating substance. The attack was to be bows-on, to take
advantage of the protective features. After the discharge, the
vessel was to back off at full speed. The stern rudder was of
a form suited to this use, and there was a second rudder under
the bow. She carried 45 tons of coal, sufficient to steam 4000
miles at 10 knots. She was one of the first twin-screw torpedo-
boats.

The Russian boats Revel and Sveaborg were built by Normand at this time (1886). They were 152 feet long and displaced 96 tons. With about 800 indicated horse-power they
made 22 and 19.7 knots respectively. They had a very good

coal capacity for their horse-power, 30 tons, and were considered very effective boats. They carried two torpedo-tubes and two rapid-fire guns.

In 1886 Schichau sent out a 144-foot boat to China under her own steam. She had twin bow tubes and four machine guns. The speed was 24.2 knots for one hour on 1597 indicated horse-power. The coal endurance was 3000 knots at economical speed.

In 1887 Yarrow built No. 80 for England. She was 135 feet long, with 105 tons displacement, 1540 indicated horse-power, and a speed of 23 knots. She carried five torpedo-tubes and four 3-pounders. She was in dimensions and performance a close approach to our Cushing.

His two boats for Italy the same year were quite similar, but made 25.1 knots, the then highest speed.

Two weeks later, the Ariete for Spain, by the Thornycrofts, made 26.1 knots, exceeding Yarrow's boat by a knot. She was 148 feet long, of 97 tons displacement and 1600 indicated horse-power. She was fitted with twin bow tubes and carried four 3-pounders. This boat exemplified all the main features of the Thornycroft construction. She had tubulous boilers, and patent double rudders outboard of the screws. The stern was flat and hollowed out underneath to give a good run of water to the screws, and to prevent squatting.

The same firm built the Coureur for France in 1887, a boat of 148 feet and 120 tons, with a speed of 23½ knots. She was regarded as a very efficient type and showed excellent sea-going qualities.

The following are extracts from the report of the Committee on Naval Manœuvres, 1888, Admiral W. M. Dowell, Chairman, as quoted by Brassey, 1888-9, page 416:

" As to ' The value of torpedo-gunboats, both with the blockading and blockaded fleets, and the most efficient manner of utilizing them.'

" Torpedo-gunboats of high speed and good coal capacity would be of incalculable value to the blockading fleet, but torpedo-boats of any class at present in use would be of far more value to the blockaded squadron than to the blockaders. Torpedo-boats, if not capable of keeping the sea independently, under all conditions of weather, would inevitably prove a cause of embarrassment and anxiety to an Admiral commanding a blockading fleet, and would be subject to endless casualties.

" First-class torpedo-boats might, with advantage, accompany a fleet if carried in a specially constructed vessel—superior class of Hecla—provided with suitable hydraulic cranes for hoisting them in and out.

" Second-class torpedo-boats, as carried in the ironclads, will, no doubt, prove useful on occasions.

" We consider, however, the new type of Vedette-boat preferable for sea-going battleships; they are better sea-boats and, being built of wood, are less liable to damage and more easily repaired than torpedo-boats.

" The balance of opinion, in which we concur, is to the effect—

" That the employment of torpedo-boats as an inner line of blockade is not desirable, they being calculated to cause much confusion and embarrassment to their friends. That they are admirably adapted for purposes of defense; but even then, without a very simple and perfect system of signals, they are liable to be taken for enemies by their own side. The documents before us show that this actually occurred once at least on each side in the course of these manœuvres.

" That torpedo-boats should not be used as despatch-vessels, or for any purpose other than that for which they are designed.

" That torpedo-nets—certainly as at present fitted—cannot be carried by vessels under weigh without impairing their efficiency and compromising their safety."

The Aquila class for Italy were built by Schichau in 1888. They were 152 feet in length and displaced 130 tons. On 2200 indicated horse-power the Aquila made 26.6 knots. The armament was three torpedo-tubes and five rapid-fire guns and revolving-cannon. The class was reported to have turned out badly in the manœuvres of that year. Strength, seaworthiness and comfort were all sacrificed to speed, which was greater than in the 128-foot type only in smooth water. This is a lesson always to be borne in mind in attempting to get more speed than the displacement and offensive features warrant. The smaller type was reverted to for awhile in Italy, though some larger boats are now proposed.

The following is from the Parliamentary Report on the English Manœuvres of 1890, as quoted in Brassey, 1891, page 26:

" The radius of action of a torpedo-boat is limited less by her coal and feed-water supply than by the physical endurance of her crew, especially of her commander. It has been assumed that the physical strain caused by continuous attention to the navigation of a boat at night cannot be supported for more than a very few hours, if the officers undergoing it are to arrive on the scene of operations still so unwearied that neither nerve, nor coolness, nor readiness of resource would be likely to fail them at a critical moment. During the late manœuvres it was proved by actual experience that there are officers who can navigate their boats for hours together across a crowded route, can reach their objective punctually at the prearranged time, and can then manœuvre at very high speed at night in an anchorage so filled with shipping that manœuvring in it when fresh and in broad daylight would require much care and attention. . . . A result of the 1890 manœuvres is, that opinions on the effective radius of torpedo-boat action will have to be reconsidered."

In 1890 Thornycroft built two very effective boats for the Argentine, the Murature and Commodoro Py. They were 150 feet long, of 110 tons displacement, 1500 indicated horse-power, and made 24½ knots. The armament was three torpedo-tubes and three 3-pounders. The Murature, on the trip out, steamed from Pernambuco to La Plata, 2300 miles, at 9½ knots with one engine, without stopping. The radius of action under these conditions is 2800 miles.

The Adler (1890), a Schichau boat for Russia, was of the Aquila type. She made 27.4 knots on trial and 26.55 for two hours. This was the highest speed to date.

Our own Cushing was launched by the Herreshoffs the same year. She is 138 feet in length, of 106 tons normal displacement, and 120 tons loaded. Her best speed was about 24 knots on the measured mile, and trial speed 22½ for three hours. This last was on 1720 indicated horse-power. Her armament is three torpedo-tubes for the short 18-inch Whitehead, and three 1-pounders. She has the exceptional bunker capacity of 39 tons, or 51 pounds per indicated horse-power, which is equivalent to a day's steaming at full spead. This feature of coal endurance is a most valuable one and will be referred to more at length in another place. She has at all times proved exceedingly safe, reliable and effective. Her sea-qualities could be somewhat improved by removing the bow torpedo-tube and building her higher forward with the weight thus saved.

Brassey's Annual, 1891, page 110, has the following:
"Experience has shown that the smaller torpedo-boats are unseaworthy. Those recently constructed in England are of about 100 tons displacement. Germany, Italy and Russia are building boats of 130 to 160 tons. It will probably be well to have torpedo-boats of two classes. The first class, of not less than 150 tons, should be able to cruise with the fleet within a certain distance from the coast. The second-class boats, for harbor defense, may be of small size and cheap construction. In the conditions which favor the attack by the torpedo-boat upon heavy ironclads blockading a port, a small and cheap type will be almost as effective as one more costly."

This last view is open to argument. The subject will be presented again when the different types of boats are discussed.

The Annual of the Office of Naval Intelligence, 1892, page 256, has this in regard to the French manœuvres of 1891:

"The most important lesson of the manœuvres, and one that has caused a deep impression, is the fact that the torpedo-boats were unable to follow the battleships at a speed of 12 knots even in moderate weather. Their small storage of coal and water, the excessive fatigue imposed on officers and men, when sleep and rest are out of the question, the impossibility often of cooking, make it necessary to resupply them and to change their crews every three or four days. The manœuvres have proved again that torpedo-boats are not fit to be attached to a squadron on a permanent footing; if it should go to sea for more than three or four days they cease to be an additional strength, but become a worry and an impediment. On the coast they have lost none of their importance; while they remain within reach of shelter, where they can be provisioned and coaled and their crews can rest, they are of the greatest value against hostile cruisers."

The boats referred to were one of 108 feet, two of 118 feet, and the remainder of 133 to 139 feet. These last boats ought to have given a better account of themselves. Still it is not a type to attach permanently to a squadron. We shall see later that a decidedly larger boat is desirable for such use.

In 1891 Thornycroft built three boats for Brazil of 150 feet and 150 tons. They had twin-screws, protected by double rudders outboard and a guard underneath, and the usual flat, hol-

lowed-out stern. They had two bow tubes and two single deck
tubes on the middle line, all for 14-inch torpedoes. They were
guaranteed to make 24 knots for two hours on 200 pounds of
steam. This they exceeded, one having made 25.4 for two hours,
but with 210 pounds of steam. The gun armament was out of
keeping with the size of the boat—two 1-pounders.

Captain Eardley-Wilmot said, in discussing a lecture before
the Royal United Service Institution by Mr. Laird Clowes in
1892:

" I quite agree with the lecturer when he says a torpedo-boat
should not be looked upon as a portion of a sea-going fleet,
although I think there is a tendency rather to make too much
about the hardships and impossibilities of existence on torpedo-
boats, because last year when the French squadron arrived at
Portsmouth Harbor they had two torpedo-boats accompanying
them, which the Admiral stated had been with him for six
months, and had been served all through the cruise by the same
officers and men, and that he found, after the first month or
two, they had gradually accustomed themselves to the life."

The Corsaire, built for the French government at St. Denis
in 1892, may be taken as the starting point of the present large,
high-speed, sea-going torpedo-boats in vogue in that country.
She is 160 feet long and displaces 150 tons. On 2500 horse-
power her speed is 25½ knots. She carries two tubes for the
long 18-inch torpedo, mounted on the central line and pivoting
on either broadside. Her gun armament is four 1-pounders.
Her coal capacity is 15 tons, which at two pounds per indicated
horse-power per hour, would last her less than seven hours at
full speed. This is a very limited coal endurance. As the indicated horse-power and speed are not high for a boat of that
size, and the armament is not excessive, the design must be
faulty; or there must be other and unnecessary weights.

In making these comparisons of coal endurance, the figure
two pounds per indicated horse-power per hour *at full speed*
has been taken as a basis. This is too low in most cases and
makes the endurance too high. Schichau, I believe, has a
record of 1.54 pounds for the Russian torpedo-gunboats Posadnik
and Woewoda on their forced-draught trials in 1893, while Normand has a record of 1.86 pounds for the Forban. The English
destroyers are required to conform to 2½ pounds under penalty

of a tax in the form of an added quantity of coal to be carried on trial. In the tables herewith there is a column for total pounds of coal carried per indicated horse-power, which, divided by the performance of the particular boat, will give the true endurance, subject to errors in the data, which may not always have come from reliable sources.

I may say in this connection that data in regard to torpedo-boats are very hard to get. The most reliable tables I know of are those given in the Naval Pocket-book of Mr. Laird Clowes, to whom I am indebted for a great deal of the information here used.

Our Ericsson dates from this time (1892). While this boat, through various unfortunate accidents, has not yet been commissioned (December, 1896), she is, as far as dimensions and power are concerned, a very perfect type of first-class torpedo-boat to operate from a shore base. She is 150 feet long, displaces 120 tons, and is to make 24 knots on 1800 horse-power. Her coal capacity is 40 tons, equivalent to 25 hours at full speed. The armament is three tubes for the short 18-inch torpedo and four 1-pounders.

The Pedro Ivo class for Brazil were built by Schichau in 1892-3. They are of the Aquila type. They crossed the Atlantic under their own steam, making the run from St. Vincent to Pernambuco under one boiler at 12 knots. They took part with the Sampaio in the attack on the Aquidaban in April, 1894, though they did no execution with their torpedoes.

In the Naval Intelligence Annual for 1894, page 57, is described the sea-test of two German torpedo-boats, S. 68 and S. 69, in February, 1894. They were boats of 144 feet and 110 tons (intermediate between the Cushing and the Ericsson) and were sent to sea from Wilhelmshaven in a gale of wind. There was a heavy swell and the wind was logged as 10 to 11. The boats behaved splendidly, kept up to the wind, lay-to, and ran before it at 16 knots with little racing. They were perfectly seaworthy and were not injured.

While the above speaks well for the boats, there is no certainty the crews could have stood such weather for long on a stretch.

The following are extracts from the official report on the English Manœuvres of 1894, as quoted in the Naval Intelligence Annual for 1895, page 194:

"The torpedo-boat operations were upon a too restricted scale to supply much valuable instruction, but as far as they went they tend to confirm the view that the most effective employment of the torpedo-boat in war will be limited to sending her to attack an enemy's ship in a known position within the boat's range of action, and that the whereabouts of the enemy must be first ascertained and be communicated to the commander of the boat. The necessity of combining with torpedo-boats vessels of other and larger classes to scout and discover the enemy, when exact information as to his position cannot be obtained by other means, seems to be established, and, if so, it carries with it the obligation to consider a mere flotilla of torpedo-boats by themselves as a belligerent factor of distinctly imperfect efficiency."

The Normand boat Chevalier for France was launched in 1893 and completed in 1894. She is of 144 feet and 118 tons. She has two Du Temple boilers in the same compartment, twin-screws, and made 27.22 knots on trial. Her horse-power is 2700, and coal consumption at full speed 1.99 pounds per horse-power. There are two 18-inch torpedo-tubes on the middle line and two 1-pounders. A novelty in the arrangement of the screws is that one is a little in advance of the other, permitting the blades to overlap. They were made to revolve in the same direction, with the idea of giving better water to the inner blades; but at high speed the boat has a decided list, due to the reaction, a feature which is of course not desirable.

In 1893-5 there were ten new boats built for the English government by Yarrow, Thornycroft, White and Laird. They varied from 140 to 142 feet, 100 to 130 tons, 1400 to 2700 horse-power, and 21 to 24 knots. Their coal capacity was 18 to 26 tons, equivalent to about 14 hours full speed for the lower horse-power and 11 hours for the higher. This is greater than in contemporary French boats, but seems inadequate to the objects to be attained, of which more later. These are the latest English boats, exclusive of torpedo-boat destroyers.

The Forban has become very celebrated by her high speed on light displacement. She was built by Normand for France in 1895 and displaces 130 tons on a length of 144 feet. Her indicated horse-power is 3250 and speed 31.2 knots. The armament is two 14-inch torpedo-tubes and two 1-pounders. Her bunker capacity is 15 tons, equivalent to an endurance of 5½ hours at full speed, allowing 1.86 pounds per horse-power, which was her performance on trial. Her tremendous horse-power and speed are thus accounted for. On a given displacement, speed, endurance, and armament contend; and one predominates only at the expense of the others. A boat of her size should carry the long 18-inch torpedoes and several rapid-fire guns of at least a 3-pounder caliber. The coal endurance might with advantage be trebled. The relative value of speed, armament and coal will be discussed in another place.

On account of the interest attaching to this boat, a few more particulars are added. The speed as given above was made at 125 tons displacement. The load displacement is 136 tons. At 130 tons, with a load of 16 tons, including coal, equipment and armament, she made 31.03 knots for one hour. It is needless to say that the above allowance of weights is preposterous for a boat of 130 tons. From reliable information, the speed is gained not only by the sacrifice of weight, but also apparently at the expense of structural strength.

One of Yarrow's latest boats is the Viper for Austria, which has been delivered within a year. She is 148 feet long and displaces 120 tons. The guaranteed speed was 24 knots with 26 tons load. She really made 26.6 for three hours on 2000 indicated horse-power. The bunker capacity is 30 tons, equivalent to 17 hours' endurance at full speed. She has only a single screw, which naturally impairs the handiness and offers greater chances for disablement. Otherwise, she is in her main features an excellent type of first-class torpedo-boat.

The United States has in course of construction fifteen torpedo-boats and one destroyer. Their principal features appear in the tables. Nos. 3 to 8 are intermediate in size to the two types which it will be seen later are thought to be desirable for our service. Their armament is light for their size, 1-pounders and short torpedoes. They would be improved by the substitution of 3-pounders and long torpedoes. Their displacement amply warrants this change.

Nos. 9 and 10 are copied after the Cyclone, a Normand boat of the Forban type slightly enlarged. The coal endurance at full speed will be about 8½ hours. The armament is to be four 6-pounders and three torpedo-tubes for the long 18-inch torpedo.

Nos. 12, 13 and 14 ought to be valuable boats. They have a heavy torpedo armament and a light gun armament. Perhaps it might be advantageous to substitute 3-pounders for the 1-pounders, saving the weight necessary by omitting one of the three torpedo-tubes. Two tubes for the long 18-inch torpedo and four torpedoes make a very fair armament for a first-class boat.

Nos. 15 to 18 are too small for general use, but are warranted by considerations of inland-water navigation and length of canal locks.

The above opinions are the result of a consideration of the relative values of speed, size, coal endurance and armaments in torpedo-boats, and anticipate a discussion at some length that appears later.

LOCATION OF TUBES IN TORPEDO-BOATS.

A number of methods of mounting tubes have been mentioned. The bow tube with steam, air or gunpowder impulse was the most common until recently. In some cases there were two of them side by side, referred to as twin tubes. This method answered fairly well when the speed was not so high as at present. Now the tube in the bow makes the boats wet in a sea-way, and it could scarcely be used except in smooth water. At high speeds there is also danger of overrunning the torpedo should it not attain its own speed quickly. By omitting these tubes, enough weight is saved to build up the bow forward and improve the sea qualities.

Tactically, the bow tube, requiring to be pointed by the helm, is not so desirable as a pivoted tube with a large angle of train. Then, too, in approaching the enemy at high speed, it is awkward to have to stop and back, or else make a wide sweep, during which the boat's broadside becomes the best possible target for the enemy. With pivoted tubes, the boat can begin the turn before delivering the first torpedo, and with a small helm can launch in succession all that will bear on one broadside, and then putting the helm hard over, can soon be out of danger.

Other methods for getting the torpedo away have been by side dropping-frames, usually from the smaller boats, already described; then from turn-table tubes on deck, singly or in pairs.

Pairs of tubes on the same turn-table have sometimes been set at a small divergent angle, with the idea of launching both torpedoes together and thus increasing the chances of hitting. They have also been laid with their muzzles in opposite directions, to permit of discharge on both broadsides. Sometimes, also, they have been mounted on racers revolving around the conning towers.

The objection generally to pairs of tubes training together is that it may not always be desired to launch both torpedoes together or on the same bearing. If one only is launched on a given bearing, it may be awkward under fire, or there may not be time to train again before the second torpedo is required. Then, too, it is desirable to have the option of training either tube separately on either beam, or both tubes on the same beam, and possibly at different angles. This cannot be done with any form of double turn-table mount.

Single tubes have been mounted near the side of the boat and on the central fore-and-aft line, in the last case with train on both beams; also on top of the forecastle and near the stern, in both positions with a large angle of train on both sides of the keel line.

Single tubes at the side are exposed to the sea, especially in the turtle-back form of construction, and in consequence it would not be advisable to install other than the smaller torpedoes in these positions. The advantages are a larger command of fire *on one broadside*. In a small boat the short tube could very well be pivoted amidships, and while thus better protected from the sea, would command a fair train *on either beam*. As the spoon is in addition to the half length of tube forward of the pivot, it reaches well over the boat's rail on whichever side it is trained.

The position on top of the forecastle, while excellent in smooth water, is open to the objection of carrying the weights high, which in itself is bad in a sea-way. Moreover, the exposed position is bad for the torpedoes on account of salt spray, and the tubes would be hard to serve with much motion on.

The stern position is also good tactically, and is not open to objections on account of weather. If, however, the torpedoes are stowed for long in tubes in this position they are affected by the vibrations due to the propellers, which are here at a maximum. If they can be stowed in other positions this objection is partially removed. On the whole, it is considered best to locate the tube where the torpedo can be kept loaded, charged and adjusted, ready for use at any time.

This reasoning points to the desirability, as a general rule, of installing the torpedoes in single tubes pivoted on the central fore-and-aft line, and at some distance from the ends of the boat. In the case of small boats, the short torpedo would be permissible, as the boat's beam would not be great enough materially to reduce the angle of train, were it not that as a type it has not been found sufficiently accurate to warrant its farther manufacture. It has been generally abandoned abroad. The standard torpedo for torpedo-boats is the long 18-inch, on account both of its greater accuracy and its larger explosive charge. While the weight is less than 30 per cent. greater than that of the short 18-inch, the gun-cotton charge is over 83 per cent. greater. The greater accuracy is due simply to its greater length, 16½ feet against 12. Two or three tubes may be carried, according to the size of the boat. The end of the spoon is 11 to 12 feet from the pivot, which takes the torpedo well clear of the side of even a large boat. By having a torpedo-carriage with the pivot towards the breech rather than the muzzle, the sweep of the spoon could be still farther increased, and angles of train exceeding 90 degrees obtained on each broadside of a boat of 20 feet beam. If a lighter torpedo is required, as for the side dropping-frames carried by vedette-launches, the long 14-inch torpedo is considered far preferable, by reason of its greater accuracy, to the short 18-inch. The explosive charges are about the same.

Smokeless powder will probably replace all other means of discharge. Air and steam require extra weight and are otherwise complicated. They are already practically replaced by gunpowder. This affords a simple means of discharge, but the pressures vary greatly with dampness. Smokeless powder gives more uniform pressures, is practically unaffected by dampness, and does not foul the tube.

MISCELLANEOUS TORPEDO-VESSELS.

The building of torpedo-vessels other than fast launches and torpedo-boats was preceded by one or two tentative types before the lines were definitely determined. Thus in 1874 the English launched the Vesuvius, which was called a torpedo-ship. She was built of iron and was 90 feet long with a displacement of 245 tons and a speed of 9.7 knots. Her armament was four submerged tubes for Whitehead torpedoes. With twin screws and coke for fuel, and the products of combustion arranged to be discharged from side holes in horizontal flues, she was intended to be handy, smokeless and noiseless. Her speed was deficient.

The Italian Pietro Micca dates from 1876. She was built of iron, was about 200 feet long and of 550 tons displacement. There was an armor deck 10 inches below the water-line with sloping sides heavily plated with steel and iron. The intended speed was 18 knots, but she did not realize over 14. She was fitted with two submerged tubes and carried ten torpedoes, besides two machine guns. She was filled with machinery and had four boilers.

The Swedes built the Ran in 1877, subsequently called the Drott. She was a twin-screw iron ship of 175 feet and 630 tons, and had a speed of 13 knots. The armament was three torpedo-tubes, one submerged, and four rapid-fire guns. She was fitted also for the Harvey torpedo.

Rather a remarkable vessel of her day was the Danish armored torpedo-ship Tordenskjold, 1880. She was a steel, twin-screw, turtle-shaped vessel, with a 3.7-inch armored deck and an 8-inch armored barbette. Her length was 222 feet, displacement 2400 tons, speed 14 knots. She had a cellular double bottom surmounted by an inner ship of forty cork-filled compartments. Above this were the armament, torpedoes and crew space. There were four torpedo-tubes, over-water, five Krupp guns of from 12 to 30 centimeters caliber and eight machine guns. She carried in addition two torpedo-boats.

A somewhat similar vessel, guns excepted, was the English torpedo-ram Polyphemus, 1881. She was a twin-screw, steel, turtle-back vessel of 240 feet and 2640 tons. Her best speed was 18 knots. The armament was five submerged torpedo-tubes, forty torpedoes, six 6-pounders and two machine guns. The steel deck was two to three inches thick. She was fitted with bow and stern rudders, and could take aboard water-ballast to sink her to just awash.

The above vessels were not reproduced, though there are possibilities in some of them. A fast armored torpedo-ram may yet be in favor, as it is not difficult to imagine cases in which such a vessel, acting singly or with the fleet, would give more than a good account of herself.

Two other types of torpedo craft may be briefly discussed here, and the way will then be clear for the cruisers, gunboats and destroyers. These are the torpedo-dépôt-ship and the German division-boat. Their principal features appear in the tables.

Of the first, the Hecla was the prototype, a British merchant steamer taken into the service and fitted for the purpose. She was followed by the Japon, the Vulcan, the Pelikan and the Foudre. The functions of the dépôt-ship were to carry spare torpedoes and stores and a large number of second-class boats to hoist out when they should be of use. They were fitted with large repair shops, and could carry relief crews for the boats as well as medical officers and stores.

The division-boat acts as the flagship of a division of torpedo-boats. It carries also spare torpedoes and stores, relief crews, medical supplies, and is fitted with repair shops, all naturally to a more limited extent than in the case of the dépôt-ships. It can be used as a scout for its division, and to a certain extent as a torpedo-boat destroyer. While these boats are about the size of the destroyers, they have not their lines or build, and the earlier ones did not have the speed. In one important feature they are very different. Their draught is 10 to 12 feet, nearly double that of the destroyers, and they are, therefore, incapable of following torpedo-boats into shoal water.

It is doubtful if either of these types can be of much value in the future. It has become apparent from the citations already made in reviewing the progress of torpedo-boats that the day of the second-class boat is perhaps past, and that first-class boats are at their best when operating from shore bases. The independent duties of the division-boats can be performed by the regular scouts or by the destroyers. Their stores and supplies will not be required by the torpedo-boats, for they will seek their own bases to renew their supplies and rest their crews; and the destroyers are capable of taking care of themselves equally with the division-boats.

The utility of the torpedo dépôt-ship disappears by the same reasoning. It may be desirable to fit up a large vessel as a floating repair shop for the whole fleet, and send her where she is most needed. The steamer Ohio, of the International Navigation Company, was to have been so fitted had we gone to war with Chile in 1892. The French Superior Council has reported against the use of the Foudre as a dépôt-ship. Plans are under discussion to convert her to a cruiser.

TORPEDO-CRUISERS.

The immediate predecessors of the torpedo-cruisers seem to have been the fast despatch-vessels which were in vogue ten to twenty years ago. The Zieten was a torpedo and despatch-vessel built by the Thames Iron Works for Germany in 1876. She was a twin-screw iron vessel of about 200 feet and 1000 tons, with a long, low hull, and bow and stern torpedo-tubes six feet under water. The designed speed was 16 knots. She carried lately 10 machine guns.

The Staffeta, built by the Italians at the same time, was 253 feet long and displaced 1388 tons. Her speed was 14 knots. She had one torpedo-tube, four 12-centimeter guns and a number of smaller ones.

The German Blitz and Pfeil, 1882, were much the same. They were twin-screw steel vessels of 246 feet and 1382 tons. Their maximum speed was 16.3 knots. Their armament was one submerged tube, besides rapid-fire and machine guns.

The Alacrity and Surprise, built by the Palmers for the English government in 1885, were purely despatch-vessels, but they gave by their lightness and speed a suggestion of possible torpedo use. They were twin-screw steel vessels of 250 feet and 1600 to 1700 tons. They made upwards of 17 knots with forced draught. The Alacrity was armed with ten 6-pounders and two machine guns. It will be seen how opinion is reverting to this style of armament for vessels of this type to the exclusion of torpedoes.

Next came the English Curlew and Landrail in 1885-6. They came very near the eventual torpedo-cruiser, but they were too small and too slow. They were twin-screw steel vessels of 195 feet and 950 tons, with a speed of 14½ knots. Their armament was a number of 5-inch and 6-inch breech-loaders, besides rapid-fire and machine guns, and three torpedo-tubes. Thus it is seen the torpedo is beginning to assume prominence

At the same time the Armstrongs were building the Leopard and Panther for Austria. They were 224 feet long, displaced 1530 tons, and had a speed of 18½ knots. They carried four torpedo-tubes in addition to a numerous gun armament. They were built with a high poop and forecastle for weatherly considerations and were much subdivided.

In the English Scout and Fearless, 1885-6, the typical torpedo-cruiser was reached. Subsequent steps have been retrogressive, at least as regards the torpedo features. They were about the size of the Leopard, but had scarcely more than half the horse-power. They were loaded down with both guns and torpedoes. They were 220 feet long, displaced 1580 tons, and steamed 16.7 knots. They carried originally eleven torpedo-tubes, one of which, in the bow, was submerged. Four have since been removed. The gun armament consisted of four 5-inch and eleven rapid-fire and machine guns. The type was intended to keep the sea in all weathers and afford comfort to the crew. They were designed as a result of the shortcomings of torpedo-boats proper, and were referred to in the prints of the day as sea-going torpedo-boats.

The French contemporaries of these vessels were the Condor and her class, the Epervier, Faucon and Vautour. Their design really preceded the English ones, but they were longer in building. They were 217 feet long, displaced 1240 tons and made nearly 18 knots. Their armament was five torpedo-tubes, and five 10-centimeter guns, besides rapid-fire and machine guns. The upper deck was turtle-backed the whole length; there was a 1½-inch steel deck, a splinter deck, a double bottom, and a cellular water-line belt. They had compound engines and four locomotive boilers.

A number of other vessels of this type followed in different countries, but it is not necessary to describe them here. Particulars of some of them are given in the tables. The English Archer, a slightly enlarged and modified Scout, and the American copy, the Yorktown, exemplified the type in the essential features. The German Greif (1886) and the Italian Coatit (1896) are the fastest of any of them, having been designed for 23 knots.

This class of vessels, as torpedo-cruisers proper, have not proved a success. They were intended to chase and destroy torpedo-boats, as well as to engage large ships with their torpedoes. They were loaded with guns, men, torpedoes and machinery. The fastest of them can catch torpedo-boats proper in deep water and in a sea-way, but they cannot follow them into shoal water. It is hard to understand in what way they were intended to use their torpedoes. They are too large to make a surprise attack. They have guns heavy enough to engage much larger and heavier vessels, but they would not dare to come near enough to use them. Stripped of their heavy guns and torpedoes, they would make very efficient scouts, especially the later and faster ones. They could carry a very numerous armament of medium-weight and light rapid-fire guns. In France this re-armament is already taking place, and markedly in the class of torpedo-gunboats, as we shall see later.

TORPEDO-GUNBOATS.

In the early days of the torpedo, the generic title of vessels expressly fitted for its use was torpedo-vessel or torpedo-ship. As the type developed, differences began to appear. Several comparatively slow vessels of various sizes retained the original name. Some of them have been described. The larger ones of moderate speed were known eventually as torpedo-cruisers, with an intermediate stage of despatch-vessels, as has been shown; and the smaller ones came to be called torpedo-catchers, and finally torpedo-gunboats.

The eventual French names of the various types, in order of size, may be given here as follows: *Croiseurs-torpilleurs, avisos-torpilleurs, éclaireurs-torpilleurs, torpilleurs de haute mer, torpilleurs-garde-côtes, torpilleurs-vedettes.*

The Austrians were the first in the field with gunboats by several years. Their Spalato and Zara, dating from 1879, were twin-screw steel vessels of 180 feet and 840 tons, with a speed of 14 knots. Their armament was a number of small caliber breech-loaders and machine guns, and two torpedo-tubes. They had a protective deck and high-speed compound engines supplied by locomotive boilers. In these regards they marked a decided advance in construction, but the speed was a disappointment.

The Sebenico (1882) and the Lussin (1883) were of the same displacement, but were slightly longer. The speed was the same. The Lussin had two 6-inch guns, besides smaller ones, and two torpedo-tubes.

The French Bombe class (1885-6) were, however, the pioneers of the typical torpedo-gunboat. The duties of this type may be summarized as follows from the Annual of the Office of Naval Intelligence, 1891, page 415: The tactical use of the torpedo-gunboat is to destroy torpedo-boats before the latter can reach the ironclads of the fleet; to cruise inside the blockading fleet and to give warning of the enemy's movements; cruising with the fleet to act as scouts, engage similar vessels, support torpedo-boat flotillas; to attack the enemy's squadron at night or force a blockade; and to undertake the duties of a high-sea torpedo-boat.

The Bombe class were twin-screw vessels lightly built of steel, 197 feet in length and of 395 tons displacement. Their speed was 18 knots, which was made with 2000 indicated horse-power. They were fitted with a water-line belt of cellulose. The sides were turtle-backed. The original boilers were of the locomotive type. They have been changed in the Bombe for the d'Allest. Nine water-tight compartments were fitted. The complement was 63 officers and men. The armament was two torpedo-tubes in the bow and seven rapid-fire and machine guns. The vessels were handy, but the construction proved too light. They rolled a great deal and were wet and uncomfortable.

The English Rattlesnake dates also from 1886. She was built of steel with a half-poop and forecastle. The length was 200 feet, displacement 550 tons. She made 19½ knots on 2800 indicated horse-power. The armament was four torpedo-tubes, one 4-inch breech-loader and six 3-pounders. There were four locomotive boilers. This type was adopted by the Board on Construction to obviate the difficulties due to wearing out of crews and constant breaking down of torpedo-boats. They were also intended to overhaul torpedo-boats in rough weather. Their light draught would ordinarily safeguard them against torpedoes.

Subsequent English types have been merely developments of the Rattlesnake. They were the Sharpshooter class, 1888-9; the Alarm or Jason class, 1892-3; and the Dryad or Halcyon class, 1893-4. Their details are sufficiently given in the tables.

The Italians entered the field with the Folgore and Saetta, 1886-7. They were 186 feet long, displaced 377 tons, and made 20 knots on 2000 horse-power. They had four torpedo-tubes and seven rapid-fire and machine guns.

The first four of the Tripoli class followed that year and the next. They were noted for their triple screws. They were much larger, reaching 845 tons and 230 feet. Their armament was five torpedo-tubes, one 4.7-inch and seven other rapid-fire guns. The speed was 20 knots on 3600 horse-power. The class has been substantially reproduced to the present time, except as to the triple screws, which were not repeated. The earlier vessels were too light and vibrated excessively. This has been corrected in later ones.

In 1886-7 Messrs. J. and G. Thomson built the Destructor for Spain. She was 193 feet long and displaced 458 tons. She made from 20 to 23 knots on 3800 horse-power, according to the load. She had four cylindrical boilers and 39 water-tight compartments, with each boiler and engine in a separate compartment. She had complete coal protection and a curved 1¼-inch steel bulkhead forward. She was cut away at the ends for manœuvring and had a bow rudder. The masts were hinged to lower. The armament was five torpedo-tubes, one 9-centimetre gun, and six rapid-fire and machine guns. She, like the Wiborg, was built for head-on attack.

It is not necessary to go farther with the descriptions. The class as such has never proved satisfactory. The size has been continually increased in the endeavor to make the vessels fast, habitable and seaworthy, until the distinctive torpedo features have practically disappeared. They have never been equal to catching the best of the torpedo-boats, a duty now relegated to the destroyers. Scouting is therefore all that is left to them. By omitting their torpedoes, other qualities can be improved, such as speed, coal endurance, gun armament and ammunition.

The French have in great measure taken this view, and the order has been given to remove the torpedoes from all the class, a work now actually in progress. The boats, however, are still to be used as catchers. All of the intermediate types between cruisers and torpedo-boats are classed as *contre-torpilleurs* in the latest published lists. The more recent and fastest of them, with a numerous armament of light rapid-fire guns, should in addition make very efficient despatch vessels and scouts.

Torpedo-boat Destroyers.

The next type of vessel to be considered is the torpedo-boat destroyer. The genesis of the type has been fairly well indicated in what precedes. The gunboats had been getting bigger and bigger, but had never been able to accomplish the object of their design, *i. e.* to catch torpedo-boats. It was decided, therefore, to build a big torpedo-boat, with plenty of engine power, and to arm her with a large number of light guns. This departure has resulted very satisfactorily. Although the destroyer was designed primarily to accompany the fleet and guard it from torpedo-boats, it was soon seen that as a high-sea torpedo-boat itself, with a moderate armament of both guns and torpedoes, it was the logical solution of the very difficult requirements of the case. This curious feature is touched on at more length in another place. The name has been retained to designate the type, but it now only partially indicates the use to which such vessels may be put. High-sea torpedo-boat would perhaps be a better designation; for it is a very good rule that any boat should have a sufficient gun armament, in addition to her torpedoes, to engage vessels of her own size and to destroy any smaller ones, which would in fact constitute her a destroyer.

The Havock, the first of the type, was built by Yarrow in 1893. She was 180 feet long, displaced 220 tons, and steamed 26.8 knots on 3500 indicated horse-power. She had three torpedo-tubes, one in the bow and two on a turn-table on deck. The gun armament was one 12-pounder on the conning-tower and three 6-pounders distributed on deck. The lines of the vessel had all the characteristics of the torpedo-boat, such as light draught, full body, sharp bow and full stern, all on an enlarged scale. Forward was a high turtle-back extending to the after side of the conning-tower. She was divided transversely by thirteen bulk-heads, and there were twenty water-tight compartments in all. The conning-tower was of ½-inch steel plates. The Havock's boilers were of the locomotive type, though her sister-boat, the Hornet, had tubulous boilers.

It is not intended to describe all of these boats. The size has increased to 210 feet and 300 tons, and the horse-power to 6000 or over, designed to give a speed of 30 to 32 knots. Some mention may be made of two or three of the most recent. The Sokol was built by Yarrow for Russia in 1895. Nickel steel was employed to lighten her construction. She is 190 feet long, of 240 tons displacement, and was guaranteed to make 29 knots on 4000 horse-power. She has triple-expansion engines and Yarrow's straight-tube boilers. The armament is two single deck tubes for 16-inch torpedoes, one 12-pounder and three 6-pounders. On her official trial, with 30 tons load, she made 29.76 knots for three hours on 3700 horse-power with an expenditure of 2.1 pounds of coal per horse-power per hour. She made 30.28 on the measured mile with 4490 horse-power, the then fastest speed.

The Desperate has just been built by Thornycroft. She is 210 feet long and displaces 272 tons. She made 30½ knots on 5600 horse-power with a coal consumption of 2.49 pounds per horse-power. The load carried was 35 tons. She broke a crosshead last June, wrecking the cylinder and scalding a number of men. She was running at 30 knots and carrying 210 pounds of steam. Our No. 11 is an essential copy of this boat, and is to make 30 knots with the same trial load, that is, 35 tons.

A departure has been made by Yarrow in four boats for the Argentine, now about completed, of which the Santa Fé is the first. They are protected by ½-inch steel armor completely surrounding the engines and boilers. The speed is 26½ knots, which means a sacrifice of three knots or more as compared with the Sokol, a vessel of practically the same size by the same firm.

This question of armor for large torpedo-boats, while advocated by some authorities, is not generally regarded with favor. The thickness of the armor is scarcely sufficient to be of much protection in an attack on a battleship or large cruiser. Surprise is here the best defense; and if this is effected, armor will not be required. In an engagement with other boats, armor might be of service, but hardly at the sacrifice of speed. An important duty of these boats is to protect the fleet from torpedo-boats. Should they fail in this through insufficient speed, the armor would be worse than useless. Taken altogether, if there is any weight that can be spared after the requisite speed and coal endurance are secured, the best place to utilize it would seem to be in added guns and ammunition.

The Durandal is one of Normand's latest boats. She is 180 feet long and displaces 300 tons. She is to make 26 knots with a load of 85 tons, representing armament, ammunition, crew, equipment, coal, and stores. The armament is two torpedo-tubes on the central line, one 9-pounder, and six 3-pounders. The full bunker capacity is 100 tons. A peculiar feature of the boat is a flying grating deck, extending from the conning-tower to within 30 feet of the stern, on which the torpedoes and guns are worked. In this boat M. Normand has remedied many of the defects noticed in the Forban type. If she meets expectations, she should prove very effective. As will be seen later, she comes very near a type that is recommended for use in our own service.

Lord Brassey, in the Annual for 1896, page 194, quotes a naval officer present at the 1895 manœuvres of the torpedo squadron as follows:

" The impression left in my mind by the manœuvres was that all the present types of torpedo-boats are obsolete, and that probably no more will ever be built. But I believe that boats of the size of the destroyers will take their place in every navy, and that a competition as regards the numbers owned will begin."

A NEW STEERING DEVICE FOR TORPEDOES.

One of the most important of the recent improvements in torpedoes, some mention of which has been made in another place, is a device for keeping the axis during the run always in the direction it had at the instant of launching. This has been accomplished both in Austria and Germany. The principle in both devices is that of a freely suspended gyroscope, which is used to bring the torpedo into its original direction through the agency of an air engine actuating a vertical rudder. The details, however, as indicated by the patent specifications, are quite different. From authentic accounts, the results of practice have been remarkable. The torpedo may be launched in any kind of weather, in any direction, from a torpedo-boat at its maximum speed by simply pointing the tube at the target. Although the torpedo is deflected as usual, the gyroscope at once brings it back to its original direction with only the error due to the short time it was off its course.

This principle is not new, as it has long been used in the Howell torpedo, but with the difference that in that torpedo the axis of the gyroscope is rigid. It, therefore, resists change of direction; but when the change has taken place, as on deflection when launched from the broadside at speed, it will not bring the torpedo back.

With the new device, the practice at a fixed target appears to be accurate even up to a range of 2000 yards. The ord working range will be easily extended beyond 1000 yards. It will always be difficult to make hits on a moving target, but it is a great gain to be able to eliminate the uncertainties of the initial deflection, hitherto the most serious drawback to accurate practice.

If it is found that the reports so far received continue to be borne out by results, it will be necessary to revise the tactics of ships as well as of boats. The value of the torpedo becomes greater than ever before, and the need of suitable torpedo-craft increases correspondingly.

SEARCH-LIGHTS IN TORPEDO BOATS.

Some of the larger torpedo-boats and destroyers are equipped with search-lights. Their utility is open to doubt. The purpose for which they are carried is to light up torpedo-boats that may be discovered and make better marks of them for the guns. At high speeds or in a sea-way, it is doubtful if a search-light can be kept on as small an object as a torpedo-boat with sufficient steadiness to make her a good target. Steady platforms are adopted for the lights in some boats, but in the absence of experience with the fittings, I doubt if they entirely overcome the difficulty. The principle is again that of the gyroscope. The relative motion of the boat with reference to the plane of the gyroscope is utilized to actuate hydraulic motors in the proper sense to keep the platform steady.

The great drawback to the search-light is that there is no concealment for the boat carrying it as soon as it is turned on, and it gradually blinds the eyes of the lookouts. Boats which would certainly be seen were the lights not used might easily get by if they happened to avoid the beam. It would appear to be better to trust to good eyesight and good lookouts to pick up the quarry; then by superior speed to stick to him until he was put out of action, aiming in the meantime as well as previous training and the circumstances would permit.

TORPEDO-DEFENSE-NETS.

The day of the defense-net is apparently passed. The objections are that they are cumbersome, hard to get in and out, cannot be carried underway except on the broadside, and then only at a greatly reduced speed, are dangerous in action from the liability to foul the propellers, could certainly not be used after an action, and might, on occasions when rigged out, prove a source of great embarrassment, due to the delay incident to getting them in.

Moreover, it was found that various devices could be fitted to the heads of torpedoes to cut through the nets. The weight· was increased to the limit of practicability and all to no purpose. Ships now building are not being fitted with them. France, Russia and Austria, I believe, have definitely abandoned them, and opinion in other countries is decidedly adverse. The United States has never adopted them. This points to the necessity of considering other means for the defense of ships against torpedo-boats.

ATTACKS UNDER THE SEARCH-LIGHT.

I purpose under this heading to examine some of the conditions under which torpedo-boat attacks may take place. The kind indicated is most generally associated with the use of torpedo-boats. As will be seen later, however, the search-light, except to a very circumscribed extent, is not recommended as a form of defense.

I will take it as established that the attack must be at least partially a surprise. With the modern batteries of rapid-fire and automatic or semi-automatic torpedo-guns, it will be impossible for the torpedo-boat to exist for more than a very limited time if she is discovered before reaching torpedo range. What that time is may well be open to discussion. It will depend on the atmospheric conditions, the amount of light on the boat, the speed of the boat, the state of the sea, the number and character of the guns that can be brought to bear, and the expertness of the gunners. The boat then must try and get as near as possible before she is discovered at all, and the ship must find a way to discover and destroy the boat before the torpedoes can be launched.

With the present development of the automobile torpedo as a weapon of war, 500 yards is the admitted effective range. Reference has been made in another place to an apparatus for steering torpedoes that seems certainly destined to revolutionize ideas in this regard, but for the present it is not considered. Now as to the best means at the disposal of the offense to bring its

vessel could be one of the fast torpedo-boats now approaching completion. She would steam directly towards the ship at her highest speed under the conditions, the ship to turn her search-lights on the target and open fire the instant the torpedo-boat passed clear on the off side. The fire would be continued until the target was estimated to be at torpedo range, after which the hits would be counted. The line could then be shortened to reduce the interval of time under fire, and the experiment be repeated. Eventually there would be some very satisfactory data connecting speed, distance, time, number and character of guns, and number of hits.

From what I have seen of somewhat similar experiments in former years, except that the target was at rest, I am under the impression that in 25 seconds, the average time of reaching torpedo range from the probable distance of discovery, as deter-mined by the Torpedo Station experiments, the torpedo-boat would not be found to be *hors de combat*. If the working range of the torpedo is materially increased by the new automatic steering device, all the arguments as above acquire added weight in proportion.

The rational defense of the ship, then, whether at anchor or underway, seems to be the scout, the torpedo-boat destroyer, the torpedo-boat, the vedette-launch, and the picket-boat. Our types of boats, then, would logically include all of the above, and, if possible, a boat adapted to evade them all. Here, per-haps, is the field for the submarine boat. This, however, opens a wide subject in itself. The essay is confined to surface boats.

DEDUCTIONS.

The various types of vessels in which torpedoes are or have been the principal arm have now been passed in review, and some of the conditions governing their use have been examined. The present tendency of opinion, as has been shown, opposes the farther development of some of them. Taking up the types in order, the conclusions that appear to be justified as regards future permissible locations of torpedoes are somewhat as follows:

The unprotected torpedo is a surprise weapon. In battle-ships and large cruisers, surprise is not attempted; but protec-tion for the torpedo may be found behind armor or in submerged positions. The protection that is deemed necessary is not to prevent explosion of the war-head, which careful experiment has shown to be a very remote contingency, but is rather to prevent destruction of the tube and mount, or explosion of the air-flask, as the result of gun-fire, before the vessel reaches torpedo range.

The only remaining questions as regards these ships are as to the numbers of tubes and their location, whether above or below water. These questions will be decided more by structural considerations and future developments of the torpedo in accuracy and ease of handling as regards over- and under-water fire. There can be little doubt that the torpedo is a desirable weapon for such ships. It has been opposed frequently on the score of its lack of reliability and the supposed danger to its users and their friends, which was regarded as comparable in degree to its menace to the enemy. Improvements in the speed, range and accuracy of the torpedo, and in the safety of handling, must counteract such of this opposition as does not spring from lack of knowledge of the weapon.

In the case of torpedo-cruisers, the justification for the presence of torpedoes at all seems to have quite disappeared. These vessels are too big to effect a surprise in any conditions of weather, and they afford no protection to the torpedoes. On discovery by a larger vessel, their only safety lies in flight. Nor are they of any use against torpedo-boats. By reason of their size they are likely to be discovered themselves before they sight the boats, a circumstance which, taken in conjunction with their lack of speed, makes the capture or destruction of the boats quite improbable.

By omitting the torpedoes and heavy guns and carrying in their place a numerous and light gun armament, and making the speed as high as the changed armament will permit, there is secured a very effective scout and lookout vessel. This is decidedly the tendency of opinion abroad to-day, and the probabilities are that in the not distant future the torpedoes will have been wholly withdrawn from the type.

Passing on to the torpedo-gunboat, or torpedo-catcher, as they are still often called, much the same reasoning obtains. This class has had a varied career from vessels of the size of the Austrian Meteor of 350 tons to the English Dryad or Halcyon of 1070. As we have seen, they are all unsatisfactory as designed. By removing their torpedoes and arming them entirely with light guns, they may be given a higher speed and thus be used as scouts and to assist the destroyers in keeping off the enemy's torpedo-boats. It is probable that the smaller ones will not be produced in the future. From the large cruiser to the present torpedo-boat destroyer, it is doubtful if there is any use for more than one type—a very fast gunboat of about 1000 tons, with a very numerous armament of medium and light rapid-fire guns and no torpedoes.

This brings us to the torpedo-boat destroyer and the torpedo-boat proper, which are now quite generally regarded as the only possible types of special torpedo craft. But when it comes to the essential features of these two types, opinions are very divergent, often, I think, due to varying conceptions of the duties of the boats in question.

This is instanced in the recent contracts for the 30-knot boats. The designs were here left to the builders. Nos. 9 and 10 as authorized are to be of 146 tons, while No. 11 is to be of 273 tons. These are odd results to follow from one clause of an appropriation act, designed to secure three essentially similar boats to carry the same armament and make the same speed. It is hard to see how the contractors for Nos. 9 and 10 are to fulfil the remaining requirements of equipment and coal supply, features in which the prototypes of these boats, as has been seen, are exceptionally deficient.

Nor would it seem to be possible that a satisfactory boat could be designed by the collective bureaus of the Navy Department that have to do with *matériel*, for the sole reason that the requirements of armament, equipment and machinery are all antagonistic to each other and to those of total displacement. If a board will first decide exactly to what use the boat is to be put, and what armament, speed, coal endurance and crew she will require for such use, then the displacement and horse-power will follow naturally. All the features will then be settled, and each bureau can have full swing in its own domain. If builders compete on their own designs, they also must use their skill within the limits of the settled requirements. If any other method is adopted in producing these boats, then when they are finished it will have to be determined what can be done with them.

I submit the following as some of the uses for which in our own case torpedo-boats will be required. I shall not say that these are the correct uses or all the uses; but the assumptions will at least lead to definite types of boats.

In the first place, boats, and a good many of them, will be needed Yor the defense of our seaports, and to operate for limited periods with the squadron near their own bases, where they can seek refuge in bad weather, leaving the Admiral entirely free of care in their regard, and can renew their supplies. These boats would be used also for massing at threatened points by means of our unrivaled inland-water communications.

Their purpose is to destroy the enemy's ships. This must be done by surprising him at night or in a fog. I leave out for a moment the case in which they attack from the lee of a battleship in action, or from a point near the scene of action, as opportunity offers. For a surprise attack at night, or in a fog, the boats should be as small as consistent with other considerations, otherwise the feature of invisibility is sacrificed. The weapon should be the equivalent of the long 18-inch Whitehead torpedo, with a speed of at least 28 knots at 800 yards and an explosive charge of 220 pounds of gun-cotton. The next smaller type sacrifices perhaps 50 per cent. of the destructive power and accuracy and reduces the value of the boat to a corresponding extent. Two at least of the torpedoes selected should be carried in central pivot training tubes on the deck of the boat, and one or more should be carried in reserve.

All torpedo-boats carry gun armaments with which to engage other boats, either for the purpose of proceeding on the intended mission or for turning back the enemy. A safe rule is to carry no less than the average armament of boats of the same size in any other service, and more if other considerations will permit. Some foreign boats carry four 3-pounders, and this is better than the average. It is a desirable armament for the purposes indicated. The automatic type of gun would be preferable should the system be found to be reliable in service. Guns of smaller caliber than 3-pounders are of little use, as it has been shown that they will not perforate the filled coal-bunkers of the ordinary torpedo-boat.

While on this subject of torpedo-boat engagements, it may be stated, as has been mentioned before, that ramming has often been recommended as a quick method of settling matters if an opportunity is afforded. If a boat or vedette can be surprised and rammed before much alarm is given, it will be a decided gain. To do this a safe rule would be to strengthen the bow of each boat to permit her to ram her own equivalent or any smaller boat. Here at once we are met by the objection that fast, handy boats cannot be turned into rams without the sacrifice of speed, that they should be built for one purpose only, and if too much is attempted, all fails.

This is a very strong argument. The only point to consider in each case when it is a question of adding some new weight is this:—is speed everything; how much speed will be sacrificed by adding this weight, and will the advantage pay for the sacrifice? To strengthen the bow of a torpedo-boat to ram one of its like or any smaller boat will require, it is estimated, 5 to 10 pounds for every ton of displacement, or for a boat of 120 tons, 600 to 1200 pounds. This would be disposed in the form of internal strengthening plates, longitudinals, and transverse braces. The loss of speed in a boat of this size per ton of added weight is estimated to be one-tenth of a knot. The weight proposed would therefore diminish the speed of the boat by the twentieth part of a knot.

While it is not claimed that the bow of a torpedo-boat thus strengthened would be absolutely uninjured by ramming, it is believed that the object would be attained without material damage. Incidentally, the boat could cut through several inches of ice without the least injury, a feature which in winter might prove of the greatest value in some of our northern ports and in the canals.

The ram form of bow is not advocated. The straight stem offers better sea-qualities and it can be made to cut as effectively as may be required. The writer saw the Richard Peck, a Long Island Sound steamer, with a straight stem, cut a tug in two halves without any apparent injury to herself. During the French manœuvres last summer, the Audacieux, a sister of the Agile, a boat the size of our Cushing, collided accidentally with the Chevalier, striking her on the side. The Audacieux's bow was wrecked, and the collision bulkhead did not stop the entrance of the water, resulting in the loss of the boat. The Chevalier had her side protected by an angle belt of steel with a wood backing, and though injured, was kept afloat. This points in the sea if more strength in the bow, whatever conclusion may be drawn as to that required in the side.

The elements of size, speed, coal endurance, and sea-keeping qualities are to a great extent interdependent. We have seen that the size cannot with advantage be great, if the boat would be too readily discovered in a surprise attack. This in itself limits the other qualities. Now the coal endurance and sea-qualities need not be greatly developed for the purposes set forth, especially the latter. When the weather is too bad for a boat of any size thus to remain at sea, it is too bad to launch torpedoes, and she may as well seek shelter.

It is somewhat different with the coal supply, as it might be necessary to return to port to coal at a very critical moment. Therefore the coal endurance, while not necessarily as great as for a sea-going boat, should not be unduly sacrificed. A week's continuous steaming at squadron speed, equivalent to 18 hours at full speed, is about the lowest point at which the endurance can well be placed. Of the boats given in the tables, the average endurance at 2 pounds per indicated horse-power per hour, is between 18 and 19 hours. This endurance can readily be obtained in a boat of 120 tons, provided excessive speed is not attempted and still an ample margin be left for the guns and torpedoes as recommended.

In this connection may be mentioned the great confusion associated with the term "normal displacement." As understood by builders, it means enough coal for the trial and as many other weights omitted as the government will permit. A rational definition of normal displacement is the displacement with all the ordnance and equipment weights aboard, the crew and their effects, and half the coal, provisions and stores that would be carried when fully loaded for sea. If it was understood that trials were to be conducted with such weights aboard as would cause the mean trial displacement to be the normal displacement as above defined, the whole question would be manifestly simplified.

As regards speed, there will be many divergent opinions. On general principles, speed is good, and it should be as high as possible. When it comes to sacrificing torpedoes, or guns, or the power to ram, or coal endurance, or involves a much increased size, then a very careful consideration should be given the relative values of the different qualities. Now what are the

objects of speed?   The first answer is, to get up to the enemy
as quickly as possible after discovery, in order that he may not
destroy you by gun-fire, and to get away from him quickly for
the same reason; secondly, to be able to strike unexpectedly
from a distance in a brief time; thirdly, to avoid the enemy's
destroyers.

In the first case suppose that 22½ and 30 knots are two speeds
to be compared.   1500 yards is a long distance at which to discover a torpedo-boat if the night is at all suited for an attack.
At 500 yards the boat can discharge her torpedoes.   The time
in passing from 1500 to 500 yards is, for the lower speed, 1 minute and 20 seconds, and for the higher speed 1 minute.   Other
things being equal, the 30-knot boat will be larger and can be
seen farther, and will afford a better target to the guns, which
will cause even this difference to vanish.   If coal endurance has
been sacrificed to accomplish speed, the sacrifice will be im-
mense, and for how small an advantage!   Moreover, torpedoes,
as at present fitted, cannot be launched with accuracy at either
of the above speeds.   The boats will have to be slowed materially on reaching the range.   Then, too, prior to discovery, it
will not be advisable to steam at more than 12 knots, to avoid
water disturbance and flame at the funnels.   When the time for
working up to full speed after discovery, and then reducing to
allow of accurate torpedo discharge is considered, there will be
a very inappreciable difference in the two boats.   In fact the
high speed boat will not have time to work up to full speed,
and the slower boat may arrive as soon.   This argument may
be modified to a certain extent by the new device that will permit torpedoes to be launched with accuracy at any speed.   But
when we consider that a boat discovered at 1500 yards is in all
probability a boat lost, if she attempts the attack, and that success depends on getting pretty close to torpedo range without
discovery at all, the argument in favor of the 30-knotter as
opposed to the boat of 22½ knots is reduced to practically nothing.   All the above to be understood to apply to the case of
the boat operating from a shore base, or with the squadron on
its own coast for limited periods.

As to being able to strike quickly from a distance, of course
the higher the speed, the better; but the difference between 30
knots and 22½ does not warrant the very considerable sacrifice
of other qualities for this purpose alone.

Now as to avoiding the destroyers in the enemy's fleet. Here
is the only approach to an argument for the higher speed. If
you can arrange that a torpedo-boat of average size with high
speed and no coal endurance shall start from port and find the
enemy without delay, she may with her speed get past the
enemy's destroyers should they sight her, provided the weather
is perfectly calm. With any sea on, the larger boats will soon
run her down. Then she must not lose any time in finding the
enemy, or her coal will be gone. It must not be lost sight of
that this speed of 30 knots or more in a comparatively small
boat is attained by sacrificing either coal, stores, or armament.
No, it looks as if the way to get past the enemy's destroyers was
to have a larger number of ordinary first-class boats, select a
dark night and make a concerted attack. Some of the boats
will be lost, but some will probably get in; and a ship or two of
the enemy will make up for losses.

As to the best type of boat, therefore, for the purpose designated, and in view of the reasoning as above stated, there is
apparently little question that a boat of 150 feet and 120 tons
would fulfil all the requirements; in other words, a boat of the
size of the Ericsson. Her contract speed is 24 knots, which is
high enough; but which could be exceeded now on the same
weights. She carries 40 tons of coal, sufficient for a day at full
speed and a week or more at 10 knots. The armament could
be improved by giving her four 3-pounders instead of three 1-
pounders, and two 18-inch torpedo-tubes for long torpedoes instead of the present three tubes for short torpedoes; the tubes to
be mounted on the central line with train on either beam. The
number of torpedoes could remain four, as at present, or two
for each tube. The difference in weight, allowing 200 rounds
of ammunition for each gun, would be 5.2 tons, of which less
than half a ton is due to the change of torpedoes and tubes.
This weight could be taken from the coal capacity, reducing the
endurance by 3½ hours; as could also 1200 pounds to fit her
bow for ramming, involving a further reduction of the endurance
by 20 minutes; but leaving it still over 20 hours.*

* The weights on which this calculation is based are as follows :—
Short 18-inch, torpedo 850 pounds, tube 1,100 pounds, mount 300 pounds,
Long 18-inch,   "   1,100   "   " 1,500   "   "   600   "
1-pounder, gun and mount 455 pounds, 200 rounds amm. boxed, 390   "
3-   "   "   "   1,610   "   "   "   "   "   1,675   "

If these boats were intended in special cases never to leave the neighborhood of their own bases, a better arrangement of the torpedoes would be to omit one torpedo and install a third tube, thus carrying three torpedoes, one in each tube. The boats would replenish their torpedoes at their bases, as required. This would involve an additional weight of 1000 pounds, which would not be prohibitive.

The next purpose to consider for which boats may be required is to accompany the fleet for indefinite periods. They may be intended to destroy the enemy's torpedo-boats or to act against his ships. For the last-named purpose the type just described would be most appropriate were it not that the endurance and sea-keeping qualities are both deficient. Near their own bases, as before shown, they may be of the greatest value. But to ensure endurance and sea qualities it is necessary to pass at once to double the displacement at least. Invisibility has to be sacrificed to ensure this ability to keep the sea with the fleet in all weathers. But granting a certain sacrifice of invisibility, it is not desirable to dispense with that quality altogether. A displacement of 250 to 300 tons can be made to produce a seaworthy boat, though perhaps not always a comfortable one. Then it is of a size that does not entirely preclude the possibility of a surprise attack on a suitable night. With this displacement it is possible to attain a satisfactory coal endurance, and in addition to increase the speed by several knots.

According to Froude's investigations, as instanced by Mr. Thornycroft in a lecture before the Royal United Service Institution in May, 1895, it is at this point that speed is more economically attained than at other displacements short of several thousand tons. This reason, and the objection to a further sacrifice of invisibility, and the desirableness of not increasing the draught beyond the requirements of shoal-water navigation, all tend to prevent a further increase of displacement. Moreover, with us, this limit is imperatively set by the dimensions of canal locks.

The argument against intermediate sizes is that for use from a fixed base they are larger than necessary, as already shown. They can be given a higher speed at the sacrifice of invisibility, but this is not desirable. For continuous use with the fleet they are not large enough to offer that guaranty of comfort and seaworthiness in all weathers deemed to be essential to the effectiveness of the crew.

With regard to the armament of these boats, the conditions already laid down make it possible to combine two objects. It was stated that the boats with the fleet were intended for use against ships or torpedo-boats. Now in the type arrived at, the considerations contemplated the first use only. But after giving the boats three torpedo-tubes, which is all they require (the recent English destroyers have two), there is still a margin of weight that can be applied to a very effective gun armament. Moreover, their high speed enables them easily to overhaul boats of the smaller type. Hence this large type is logically capable of both uses, or of any use to which boats with the squadron may be put; either to destroy the enemy's ships when opportunity offers, or to defend the squadron against the enemy's torpedo-boats.

It is curious to notice that the actual differentiation of this type, destroyers as they are called, was quite different. They were built originally to catch torpedo-boats. They were to be large enough and have speed enough to overtake torpedo-boats in rough or smooth water, and were to be able to follow them into shoal water. They were to carry a powerful gun armament, sufficient to destroy any torpedo-boat. At first even it was not contemplated to give them torpedoes. But as they would then have been harmless against large ships, and would have had no weapon with which to defend themselves, it was decided to arm them with a few torpedoes also. It has been shown that they are able to carry both guns and torpedoes. After several years' experience with the type, it appears that they are just what is required for general use with the fleet. Thus, more or less by accident, a type has been developed which a logical consideration of the requirements indicates to be the only one admissible.

The armament of the latest English destroyers is two torpedo-tubes for the long 18-inch Whitehead, one 12-pounder rapid-fire gun, and five 6-pounders. Spare torpedoes are also carried. I believe these boats would suit our purposes better were another tube added, and the gun armament changed to eight 3-pounders. The boat would then go into action with three torpedoes ready for launching, and with a light and numerous homogeneous battery of rapid-firers. The automatic type of gun is to be preferred. The weight saved by this change I estimate to be two tons, a part of which could go to supplying enough torpedoes to make two for each tube, and the rest to extra ammunition for the 3-pounders.

As to other types of torpedo-boats than those heretofore considered, it has been shown that a farther increase of size is not permissible. Can a smaller type than either of the above ever be of use? It may be answered that with all the conditions favorable, smaller boats may sometimes make successes. But in view of the great limitations to their use, it is not the part of policy to include them as standards of type. There may be limiting considerations of draught of water and length of canal locks that will determine a type of boat, in which case the limitations have to be observed. Ordinarily the power of offense, sea qualities, coal endurance and speed would be reduced to a point that would result in an unsatisfactory boat.

Much has been written in regard to the place of the torpedo-boat in a fleet action. It has been assumed in the present essay that the squadron on its own coast would be attended by both torpedo-boats and destroyers. In case it is found desirable to employ torpedo-boats in an action at sea, are the two types recommended suitable for such use, or should there be still a third type for this purpose alone? The only methods that have been much advocated are for the boats to keep in the line, each one on the off side of a battleship; or for them to haul out at the beginning of the action and watch a chance to fall on a partially disabled or otherwise occupied enemy.

In the first case the boats should be small and handy, ready to dart out at any moment to take advantage of smoke, should there be any, or such cover as their own or disabled ships of the enemy might offer. In the second case speed would be the great desideratum. Two or three boats might strike suddenly at an enemy that had been compelled to leave the line, either temporarily or permanently. Here, also, boats would be required to act on the defensive and protect disabled ships of their own line from the attacks of the enemy's boats.

Although it has sometimes been advocated that torpedo-boats should make concerted attacks on the enemy's line by day, prior to beginning an action, I cannot conceive of such an attack by a sane commander, except in case of fog or mist, which would liken the conditions to those of night-time.

For any of the above uses, torpedo-boats and destroyers of the types already recommended would seem to be the choice in preference to other possible types. In fact the determining requirements of armament, invisibility, sea qualities, speed, and endurance are precisely the same, and would therefore in natural course produce the same results.

As to second-class torpedo-boats for carrying on shipboard, the weight of opinion is not in favor of them. There might be circumstances in which they could be lowered and sent against the ships of an enemy at anchor and near-by, or in fine weather when about to pass a known point. But it is not to be supposed that the enemy will be unprovided with torpedo-boats or destroyers, which would make quick work of the second-class boats. Again, should the weather come on bad while the boats were away, they would be a great source of uneasiness to the squadron. In a fleet action they would be shot to pieces if left in their cradles, and if the weather was bad it would be equally unsafe to lower them. Then, too, if the fleet is properly provided with torpedo-boat destroyers when cruising at a distance, and with first-class boats when 'near home ports, the second-class boats will not be required.

There seems to be a need, however, of a sufficiently large and fast ship's boat to act as a vedette. The larger ships could carry one or two of them. With the squadron at anchor in striking distance of the enemy's torpedo-boats, these vedette-launches would form a line of defense inside the torpedo-boats and destroyers. They need not carry torpedoes at all for this purpose, but would be armed with a couple of rapid-fire guns and would be well provided with signal rockets. Torpedoes in fact would be a disadvantage, as they would interfere with the gun armament. The use of torpedoes against torpedo-boats is not feasible, on account of the difficulty of hitting a fast-moving target. Also torpedoes set for ships would pass under them.

For purposes such as the above, a fast wooden launch of 50 to 60 feet, capable of steaming 17 knots and carrying two light guns, would meet all the requirements. Wood seems to withstand rough usage better than thin steel. The boats have more elasticity and can be handled with fewer precautions. They are also more easily repaired when damaged. A boat like this would be useful in many other ways aboard ship, especially when the anchorage was distant from the landing. They would have to take their chances in an action with the other ships' boats. All would probably be lowered and left to their fate, or to be picked up by the victors.

The English fit these boats with side dropping frames for torpedoes. The frames are removable and are not ordinarily carried. This is perhaps the only feasible way of using torpedoes from ships' boats in the few cases in which they would be required. The short 18-inch torpedo, or baby Whitehead, as it was called, was originally used in these boats; but lately the long 14-inch has been substituted on account of its greater accuracy. The weight of gun-cotton in the two torpedoes is practically the same.

The internal arrangements of the boats reviewed were not described. There is a feature, however, that warrants mention, the disposition of engines and boilers as regards safety against disablement. Twin screws are desirable as a matter of course, though a number of foreign boats do not have them. They make the boat handier and lessen the chance of a complete breakdown. By disposing the engines one in advance of the other in separate water-tight compartments, and protecting them by coal-bunkers at the sides, the chances of complete disablement are much reduced. In some foreign boats the engines are side by side with no coal outboard of them, a practice certainly not to be desired. For similar reasons the boilers should be in separate compartments.

Some foreign nations, notably the Italians, have experimented for a long time with liquid fuel. There is perhaps no one feature that can be made of more value to torpedo-boats. The advantages to be gained are greater endurance for the same weight, greater facility for renewing fuel, absence of smoke, more regular steam, and less attendance. This last advantage involves a saving in weight and space that may be applied to an increase of either speed, endurance or armament on the same displacement. Added to these advantages, that we have in this country a practically unlimited supply of petroleum oils, which can be stored for use at the torpedo bases, and carried in the larger ships for the use of the torpedo-boats, that is until such time as the ships themselves are fitted to burn it, when it can be drawn from their tanks, and the argument for an early resort to liquid fuel seems unanswerable.

Since the above was written it is noted that the Secretary of the Navy in his annual report states that in consequence of the satisfactory results of the recent trials of liquid fuel in the Maine's torpedo-launch, farther experiments are to be made in a tug now building at Norfolk and in one of the smaller boats contracted for by the Herreshoffs.

Leaving the question of torpedo-boats, there is one other type that may be briefly referred to again—the torpedo-ram. A vessel a little larger and a little faster than the Katahdin, and fitted with several submerged broadside tubes, something after the fashion of the Polyphemus, might prove a valuable adjunct to the fleet. The turtle-back upper works could be made impregnable to the projectiles of rapid-fire guns. By watching her chances and rushing in at an opportune moment, using either torpedoes or ram as circumstances indicated, she might very well score an important success.

RECAPITULATION.

The conclusions here arrived at may be summarized as follows:

Torpedoes are not permissible afloat except in large ships, submerged or behind armor, and in special torpedo-craft of less than 300 tons displacement.

There are only two types of torpedo-boats that seem to meet the requirements of torpedo service with the squadron at sea; and, from fixed bases, for the defense of the seaports and harbors of the coast.

The first is a high-sea torpedo-boat of 250 to 300 tons, generally similar to the present English destroyers, to mount three long 18-inch torpedo-tubes on the central fore-and-aft line, with a spare torpedo for each tube, and a homogeneous battery of eight 3-pounders, preferably of the automatic type; this boat to keep the sea with the fleet at all times and to be used either as torpedo-boat or destroyer. The speed and coal endurance are to be as high as the displacement and armament of the boat will permit.

The second type is a first-class torpedo-boat of 150 feet and 120 tons, carrying two or three torpedo-tubes according to circumstances, as previously indicated, all for the long 18-inch torpedo, and mounted on the central fore-and-aft line. In case two tubes are carried there will be a spare torpedo for each tube; if three tubes, then one torpedo only for each tube. The gun armament to be four 3-pounders. A speed of 24 knots will be ample for this boat, and will permit of a coal endurance of at least 18 hours at full speed.

Both types should have twin screws and the engines should be in separate compartments longitudinally to minimize the risk of complete disablement, and to permit coal protection throughout the machinery space.

The bows of the boats should have sufficient strength to cut into the sides of any similar boat, or to permit running over a vedette-launch; which incidentally would enable them to cut through several inches of ice without injury, a feature of some value for inland-water navigation in the winter.

For each of the battleships and armored cruisers, it would be desirable to provide one or two wooden vedette-launches of 50 to 60 feet in length to steam 17 knots, to be armed ordinarily with two light guns, or, as an alternate on special occasions, with a smaller type of torpedo carried in removable frames.

The proportion of the two types of torpedo-boats could very well be one of the larger to two of the smaller; and that number would be a suitable proportion to each battleship and armored cruiser. These boats could be authorized at the rate of a dozen a year until the full number was reached, and thereafter it would be the part of policy to provide for a destroyer and two torpedo-boats whenever a large ship was laid down.

May it be permitted at the close of this paper to make a sentimental plea for naming instead of numbering torpedo-boats? The general practice abroad is to number the smaller boats, though this is not invariable, and usually to name the larger ones. Boats of the size of those here recommended are almost always named. I cannot think of any possible reason for not naming our boats, unless it is that if we have very many, the names may give out. That time has certainly not yet arrived. One disadvantage of numbers is that they are easily confused in orders and reports. For that reason cable codes make use of names to represent numbers.

But after all, the real reason for naming the boats is a sentimental one. If officers and men are willing to risk their lives in a torpedo attack, and honestly prefer to serve in a boat with a significant name instead of an insignificant number, their wishes ought to be considered.

TORPEDO-BOATS.

Name.	Date.	Builder.	Nation.	Length.	Tons.	I. H. P.	Speed.	Coal.	Lbs. per I. H. P.	Guns.	Tubes.
Miranda	71	Thornycroft	Yacht	50	...	....	16.2	....	..	....	......
Wasp	73	"	Norway	57	16	90	17.2	2	50	....	......
Boat	74	Yarrow	Argentine	55	...	65	12.5	...	..	....	......
Flint	75	Thornycroft	Sweden	58	...	60	18	1.5	56	1 M.	1
Lightning	76	Herreshoff	U. S.	58	3	....	17.6	...	..	......	......
Vitana	76	Thornycroft	Yacht	86	29	450	20.7	....	..	......	......
Lightning	77	"	England	84	27	460	19.4	....	..	....	1
Nos. 17, 18	77	Yarrow	"	86	33	450	21	7	35	....	2
No. 14	78	"	"	87	33	550	21.9	7	29	....	2
Several	78	Various	France	108	45	400	19	10	56	2 1-Pd.	2
Boat	79	Herreshoff	England	60	8	...	16	...	..	....	.....
Boats	79	Yarrow	Japan	100	40	620	20	3	11	....	......
No. 10	80	Thornycroft	England	90	28	450	22	...	..	....	1
Satoum	80	Yarrow	Russia	100	40	500	22	10	45	2 R. C.	2
Svaerdfisken	81	Thornycroft	Denmark	110	50	600	20	10	37	1 "	2
Boat	82	Yarrow	Italy	100	...	500	22.5	10	45	....	2
Boats	82	Schichau	"	100	40	620	22	10	36	1 R. C.	2
Lookhum	83	Thornycroft	Russia	113	64	700	19.5	10	32	2 "	2
Poti	83	Normand	"	125	72	570	18.5	11	43	2 "	2
3 Boats	{83}{90}	Schichau	Germany	{121}{128}	{85}{88}	1000	{19}{22}	....	..	2 R. C.	2
Swift	85	White	England	150	125	1300	20.8	35	60	6 3-Pd.	2
Falke	85	Yarrow	Austria	135	95	1250	22.4	28	50	2 M.	2
Boats	85	Stettin	Greece	128	85	1050	19	20	43	4 R. C.	......
7 Boats	85-6	T., W., Y.	England	{113}{128}	{60}{75}	{600}{1000}	{18}{22}	{10}{20}	{37}{45}	2 3-Pd.	{1}{5}
Salny	86	Normand	France	135	70	700	20	12	38	2 R. C.	2
Kotaka	86	Yarrow	Japan	170	190	1400	19	50	80	4 M.	6
Viborg	86	Thomson	Russia	142	142	1400	20.6	45	72	2 R. C.	3
Level	86	Normand	"	152	96	800	22	30	84	2 R. F.	2
Boat	86	Schichau	China	144	...	1597	24.2	....	..	4 M.	2
No. 80	87	Yarrow	England	135	105	1540	23	30	44	4 3-Pd.	5
Boats	87	Italy	Italy	135	110	1600	24	30	42	{1 1-Pd.}{1 R. C.}	5
Boats	87	Yarrow	"	140	100	1600	25.1	30	42	{2 3-Pd.}{1 R. C.}	5
Riete	87	Thornycroft	Spain	148	97	1600	26.1	25	35	4 3-Pd.	2
Coureur	87	"	France	148	120	1550	23.5	22	32	4 M.	2
Boats	88	"	Denmark	138	95	1200	22.5	15	28	2 1-Pd.	4
Larme	88	St. Nazaire	France	151	148	1400	20.5	40	64	2 3-Pd.	4
Aquila	88	Schichau	Italy	152	130	2200	26.6	40	41	{2 3-Pd.}{2 1-Pd.}{1 R. C.}	3
Kile	89	La Seyne	France	139	103	1100	20.4	14	29	3 3-Pd.	2
Boats	89	Creusot	Japan	115	56	525	20	....	..	2 1-Pd.	2
Boats	{89}{90}	Gaarden	Turkey	127	85	1300	22	20	34	2 R. C.	2
Aurature	90	Thornycroft	Argentine	150	110	1500	24.5	22	33	3 3-Pd.	3
Adler	90	Schichau	Russia	152	130	2200	27.4	....	..	....	2
Cushing	90	Herreshoff	U. S.	138	106	1720	24	39	51	3 1-Pd.	{2}{1 18" S.}
Boats	91	Schichau	Japan	125	90	1300	23	24	41	....	3
Boats	91	Thornycroft	Brazil	150	150	1800	25.4	22	27	2 1-Pd.	{4}{14"}
Dragon	92	Normand	France	138	119	1400	25	16	26	3 3-Pd.	2
Corsaire	92	St. Denis	"	160	150	2500	25.5	15	13	4 1-Pd.	{2}{2 18" L.}
Ericsson	92	Dubuque	U. S.	150	120	1800	24	40	50	4 1-Pd.	{3}{3 18" S.}
Pedro Ivo	92-3	Schichau	Brazil	152	130	2200	26	30	31	2 1-Pd.	3
Mansquenet	93	Nantes	France	165	138	2800	24.5	18	14	2 1-Pd.	2
Mousquetaire	93	Graville	"	154	125	2100	24.8	18	19	2 1-Pd.	{2}{2 18" L.}
Chevalier	93	Normand	"	144	118	2700	27.2	17	14	2 1-Pd.	{2}{2 18" L.}

TORPEDO-BOATS.—*Continued.*

Name.	Date.	Builder.	Nation.	Length.	Tons.	I. H. P.	Speed.	Coal.	Lbs. per I. H. P.	Guns.	Tubes.
10 Boats	93-5	Y., T., W., L.	England	{ 140 { 142	100 130	1430 2690	21 24	18 26	28 } 22 }	3 3-Pd.	3
5 Boats	93-4	Schichau	Germany	144	125	2500	25	....	..	2 R. C.	3
19 Boats	93-5	....	Italy	131	85	1000	22	7	16	2 1-Pd.	2
4 Boats	94	Schichau	China	...	120	....	24.5	....	..	2 R. F.	2
Aquilon	95	Normand	France	138	120	2000	26.2	17	19	2 3-Pd.	2
8 Boats	95	Schichau	Germany	144	140	1500	22	....	..	2 R. C.	3
Forban	95	Normand	France	144	130	3250	31.2	15	10	2 1-Pd.	2 14″
Viper	95	Yarrow	Austria	148	120	2000	26.6	30	34	....	2
6 Boats	95-6	....	Russia	138	118	...	25	.	.	....	2
5 Boats	96	....	France	121	80	1500	24	14	21	2 1-Pd.	2
Mangini	96	Nantes	"	147	129	2100	25	17	18	2 3-Pd.	2
1 Boat	96	....	China	137	120	1250	20	....	.	2 3-Pd.	2
4 Boats	96	....	Spain	147	97	1600	25	25	35	....	2
Natter	96	Schichau	Austria	151	150	2268	26.5	30	30	2 3-Pd.	3
Cyclone	Bldg.	Normand	France	...	148	3500	31	....	..	....	.....
Nos. 3, 4, 5	"	{ Columbian { Iron Works	U. S.	160	142	2000	24.5	50	56	3 1-Pd.	{ 3 { 18″ S
Nos. 6, 7	"	Herreshoff	"	175	180	4000	27.5	68	38	4 1-Pd.	{ 3 { 18″ S
No. 8	"	Moran Bros.	"	170	182	3200	26	60	42	4 1-Pd.	{ 3 { 18″ S
Nos. 9, 10	"	{ Bath { Iron Works	"	147	146	4200	30	32	17	4 6-Pd.	{ 3 { 18″ L.
Nos. 12, 13	"	{ Wolff & { Zwicker	"	146	117	1750	22.5	25	32	3 1-Pd.	{ 3 { 18″ L.
No. 14	"	Herreshoff	"	140	103	1750	22	28	36	3 1-Pd.	{ 3 { 18″ L.
Nos. 15, 16	"	"	"	100	47	850	20	....	..	1 1-Pd.	{ 2 { 18″ S.
No. 17	"	Chas. Hillman	"	102	65	850	20	16	42	1 1-Pd.	{ 2 { 18″ S.
No. 18	"	{ Columbian { Iron Works	"	102	65	850	20	16	42	1 1-Pd.	{ 2 { 18″ S.

MISCELLANEOUS VESSELS.

Name.	Date.	Where Built.	Nation.	Length.	Tons.	I. H. P.	Speed.	Guns.	Tubes.
Vesuvius	74	....	England	90	245	350	9.7	None.	4
Pietro Micca	76	....	Italy	203	550	1400	14	2 M.	2
Drott	77	Stockholm	Sweden	175	630	900	13	4 R. F.	3
Hecla	78	Belfast	England	392	6400	2400	11.7	{ 6 40 to 64 Pds. } { 14 Machine. } { 5 Torp. Boats. }	5
Japon	..	....	France	315	3400	1500	11.2	2 Small.	..
Tordenskjold	80	Copenhagen	Denmark	222	2400	2600	14	{ 1 30 cm, 2 15 cm, } { 2 12 cm, 8 M. }	4
Polyphemus	81	Chatham	England	240	2640	5500	18	6 6-Pd., 2 M.	5
Division Boats	{ 87 { 95 }	Elbing	Germany	{ 185 { 213	250 380	1800 4000	21 } 26 {	6 R. F. & R. C.	3
Vulcan	89	Portsmouth	England	350	6620	12000	20	{ 37 R. F. & M. } { 6 Torp. Boats. }	6
Pelikan	91	Elbing	Austria	279	2440	4700	18.3	{ 2 6-in., 8 R. F., } { 36 Torpedoes. }	..
Foudre	95	Bordeaux	France	371	6100	11400	19	{ 16 R. F. } { 10 Torp. Boats. }	4

DESPATCH-VESSELS AND TORPEDO-CRUISERS.

Name.	Date.	Where Built.	Nation.	Length.	Tons.	I. H. P.	Speed.	Guns.	Tubes.
Zieten	76	Blackwall	Germany	197	975	2350	16	10 M.	2
Staffeta	76	Sampierdarena	Italy	253	1388	1900	14	4 12 cm, 11 Small.	1
Blitz	82	Kiel	Germany	246	1382	2800	16.3	14¾″, 4 3¾, 4 M.	1
Alacrity	85	Jarrow	England	250	1700	2800	17.8	10 6-Pd., 2 M.	..
Curlew	85	Devonport	"	195	950	1200	14.5	1 6″, 3 5″, 7 M.	3
Leopard	85	Elswick	Austria	224	1530	6000	18.5	2 12 cm, 10 R. F. & M.	4
Scout	85	Clydebank	England	220	1580	3200	16.7	4 5″, 11 R. F. & M.	(11) 7
Condor	85	Rochefort	France	217	1240	3600	17.7	5 10 cm, 7 R. F. & M.	5
Infanta Isabella	85	Cadiz	Spain	210	1152	1500	14	4 4.7″, 4 6-Pd., 1 M.	2
Greif	86	Gaarden	Germany	318	2000	5400	23	3 3.9″, 10 R. C. & M.	..
Milau	86	St. Nazaire	France	303	1546	4132	18.4	5 3.9″, 8 1 Pd.	2
Archer	86	Clydebank	England	225	1770	3500	16.5	6 6″, 11 R. F. & M.	8
Coreetz	86	Stockholm	Russia	206	1213	1500	13.5	2 8″, 16″, 8 R. F. & R. C.	2
Dogali	86	Elswick	Italy	260	2000	7600	19.7	6 6″, 15 R. F.	4
Tiger	87	Triest	Austria	231	1641	6000	19	4 4.7″, 10 R. F.	4
Archimede	87	Venice	Italy	230	784	1700	16	4 4.7″, 4 R. F. & R. C.	2
Wacht	87	Bremen	Germany	279	1240	4000	20	4 3.4″, 2 M.	3
Isla de Cuba	87	Elswick	Spain	185	1040	2627	16	4 4.7″, 8 R. F. & M.	3
Yorktown	88	Philadelphia	U. S.	230	1700	3660	17.2	6 6″, 9 R. F., R. C. & M.	(8)
Cosmao	89	Bordeaux	France	312	1877	6300	20.5	4 5.5″, 7 3-Pd.	5
Barracouta	89	Sheerness	England	220	1580	3000	16.5	6 4.7″, 6 R. F. & M.	2
Barham	89	Portsmouth	"	280	1830	4700	18.6	6 4.7″, 6 R. F. & M.	2
Falke	91	Kiel	Germany	256	1580	2800	15.5	8 3.9″, 4 1-Pd.	1
Wattignies	91	Rochefort	France	233	1310	4200	18.6	5 3.9″, 13 R. F. & R. C.	4
Kondor	92*	Hamburg	Germany	246	1640	2700	16.5	8 3.9″, 5 R. C.	2
Coatit	Bldg.	....	Italy	...	1313	....	23	....	..

TORPEDO-GUNBOATS.

Name.	Date.	Where Built.	Nation.	Length.	Tons.	I. H. P.	Speed.	Guns.	Tubes.
Spalato	79	Triest	Austria	180	840	1000	14	4 9 cm, 8 Small.	2
Sebenico	82	Pola	"	187	840	1200	14	Ditto.	1
Lussin	83	Triest	"	200	840	1000	14	2 15 cm, 8 Small.	2
Bombe	85	Havre	France	197	395	2000	18	7 R. F. & R. C.	2
Rattlesnake	86	Birkenhead	England	200	550	2800	19.5	1 4,″ 6 3-Pd.	4
Folgore	86	Castellamare	Italy	186	377	2000	20	7 R. F. & M.	4
Tripoli	86	"	"	230	845	3600	20	1 12 cm, 7 R. F.	5
Destructor	86	Clydebank	Spain	193	458	3800	20.2	1 9 cm, 6 R. F. & M.	5
Ilyen	86	....	Russia	230	600	3550	20.1	13 R. F. & R. C.	7
Meteor	87	Elbing	Austria	187	350	3500	23	9 3-Pd.	4
Sharpshooter	88	Devonport	England	230	735	3500	19.6	2 4.7,″ 4 3-Pd.	5
Planet	89	Jarrow	Austria	210	500	3500	19.6	10 R. F.	3
Temerario	89	....	Spain	190	570	2600	20	2 12 cm, 5 R. F. & M.	2
Espora	90	Birkenhead	Argentine	210	615	3500	20	7 R. F. & M.	5
Condell	90	"	Chile	230	750	4350	20.3	{ 3 14-Pd. { 4 3-Pd., 2 M. }	5
Meteor	90	Gaarden	Germany	262	946	4500	21	4 R. F.	3
Kazarsky	90	Elbing	Russia	190	400	3500	22	9 R. F.	2
Léger	91	Lorient	France	197	450	2230	18.8	1 10 cm, 7 R. F.	3
Filipinas	92	Cadiz	Spain	233	747	4500	20	2 12 cm, 8 R. F. & M.	4
Alarm	92	Sheerness	England	230	810	3500	19.2	2 4.7,″ 4 3-Pd.	3
D'Iberville	92	St. Nazaire	France	262	925	506	21.6	1 10 cm, 7 Small.	6
Gustavo Sampaio	93	Elswick	Brazil	196	500	2300	18	2 20-Pd., 4 3-Pd.	3
Satellit	93	Elbing	Austria	220	500	4900	22.5	9 3-Pd.	..
Speedy	93	Chiswick	England	230	810	4500	20	2 4.7,″ 4 3-Pd.	3
Dryad	93	Chatham	"	250	1070	3700	18.5	2 4.7,″ 4 6-Pd.	5
Patria	93	Birkenhead	Argentine	250	1183	5000	20.7	{ 2 4.7,″ 4 8 Pd. { { 2 3-Pd., 2 M. }	5
Cassini	94	Havre	France	262	958	5000	21	13 R. F.	3
Caprera	94	Leghorn	Italy	230	853	4250	19.8	{ 1 12 cm. { 4 6-Pd., 2 1-Pd. }	4
Magnet	96	Elbing	Austria	221	473	3700	26	6 3-Pd.	3
Dunois	Bldg.	Cherbourg	France	256	896	6400	23	12 R. F.	..
Molinas	"	....	Chile	295	1200	....	...	14 R. F., 2 M.	4

TORPEDO-BOAT DESTROYERS.

Name.	Date.	Builder.	Nation.	Length.	Tons.	I. H. P.	Speed.	Coal.	Lbs. per I. H. P.	Guns.	Tubes.
Havock	93	Yarrow	England	180	220	3500	26.8	57	36	{ 1 12-Pd. }	
Hornet	93	"	"	180	220	4600	27.3	57	28	{ 3 6-Pd. }	3
Daring	93	Thornycroft	"	185	220	4842	28.6	50	23	Ditto { 2 12-Pd. }	3
29 Boats	93-5	Various	"	{ 190 { 200	220 280	3200 4800	27 29	60 70	42 33	{ 3 6-Pd. { 1 12-Pd. { 5 6-Pd.	{ 3 { 2
7 Boats	94-5	Laird	"	210	{ 265 { 300	4400 6000	27 30	..	..	Ditto	2
Sokol	95	Yarrow	Russia	190	240	4490	30.3	60	30	{ 1 12-Pd. { 3 6-Pd.	2
Desperate	96	Thornycroft	England	210	272	5600	30.5	..	..	{ 1 12-Pd. { 5 6-Pd.	2
4 Boats	96	Laird	Chile	210	300	6000	30	..	..	Ditto	2
Sante Fé	96	Yarrow	Argentine	190	250	4000	26.5	80	45	{ 1 14-Pd. { 3 6-Pd. { 2 M.	3
Furor	96	Thomson	Spain	220	380	6200	28.2	..	..	{ 2 14-Pd. { 2 6-Pd. { 2 M.	2
Durandal	Bldg.	Normand	France	180	300	....	26	100		{ 1 9-Pd. { 6 3-Pd.	......
No. 11	"	{ Union { Iron Works	U. S.	210	273	5600	30	..	..	4 6-Pd.	3

DISCUSSION.

Lieutenant E. W. EBERLE, U. S. Navy.—I have read with much interest the paper by Lieutenant R. C. Smith, U. S. N., entitled " Torpedo-Boat Policy," and it is a very instructive history of the evolution of the torpedo-boat.

I agree with the policy of the essayist in attaching great importance to the torpedo-boat, especially in harbor defense, but I regret that he did not designate the swift ram as the " running mate " of the torpedo-boat in this noble work of " aggressive defense." Of equal importance is the torpedo-boat destroyer, its duty being principally with the fleet along the enemy's coast, or upon the adjacent sea to insure the battle-ship against surprise by torpedo-boats.

My opinion is that the appropriation for each battle-ship or armored cruiser should contain a provision for two torpedo-boat destroyers. These two " destroyers " should attend the battle-ship during all manœuvres, and in time of hostilities they should serve as her " faithful watch-dogs " at night, being always on the alert for torpedo-boats and rams. The service that these " destroyers " could render a fleet of fighting ships would prove most valuable—some on the scout and others on the lookout. They could form an inner picket line for the fleet, the outer line being formed by the large cruising scouts. How much more

secure and comfortable the fighting ships would feel, when on the blockade or when approaching the enemy's coast, if each one had two effective ✦
torpedo-boat destroyers to insure protection from the ever-dreaded little
" night-prowling " torpedo-boats. The two " destroyers " should be a
" part and parcel " of the battle-ship and under the orders of her commanding officer; and they should look to the battle-ship for all supplies
when cruising and also for protection from the enemy's fighting ships.
During action they could often find safety under the unengaged side
of their powerful protector and be ever ready to dart forth to repel the
onslaught of torpedo-boats. To each coast-defense vessel should be
attached one " destroyer " in addition to the number of torpedo-boats
that should always accompany a fleet of coast defenders. Thus, for
example, a fleet of six monitors should have six " destroyers " and probably eight torpedo-boats and two rams; the " destroyers " would act as
scouts and as protectors against the " destroyers " or torpedo-boats of
the enemy.

Torpedo-boats should never put to sea excepting to go to the assist-
ance of an engaged fleet a few miles off the coast in comparatively
smooth weather; they are really " pure and simple " harbor defenders,
and in this valuable service they should always have the rams as their
companions.

I think that we have seriously overlooked the great importance of the
ram and torpedo-boat in harbor defense. For the purpose of illustration, take the harbor of San Francisco and assume that it has no forti-
fications whatever, no mines and no torpedoes in its approaches; but let
the enemy be aware that within that harbor are about ten torpedo-boats
and several rams and " destroyers." Would any commander-in-chief
dare enter that harbor with his battle-ships and cruisers? Would he
not realize that these little " night-hawks " and rams were hiding in
every cove and behind every island within that large bay, ever ready
to dart forth at his powerful fighting ships in the darkness or fog and
then run for cover behind the many inviting islands? I do not believe
that any commander-in-chief would dare imperil his fleet by entering
such a harbor, or at least not until he should send in his " destroyers "
and they prove capable of driving the little defenders into the shoal
waters of upper San Francisco Bay for safety—a somewhat difficult feat
to accomplish.

What is true of San Francisco Bay is true of many harbors on our
eastern coast, and the illustration goes to prove that torpedo-boats and
rams are very important in the defense of harbors, and at the same time
it shows that the only way to overcome such opposition would be to
have a large number of " destroyers " with the fleet.

I consider the ram to be as important in harbor defense as the torpedo-boat, and they should always be associated; and the ram should
also be an important factor in the cruising or in the blockading fleets.

The " moral effect " that torpedo-boats and rams would have upon
the enemy would alone be sufficient remuneration for their maintenance;
they would prove a constant source of worry to commanders of fighting

ships, because it is realized that these little vessels are ever ready to dart through the darkness and sacrifice themselves in attempts on the life of the huge battle-ships, and though unsuccessful in the attack, the sacrifice is praiseworthy.

In my opinion, torpedo-boat destroyers should be well-built swift vessels of at least 300 tons displacement, of large coal capacity, and with an armament of one twelve-pounder and five six-pounders, or one twelve-pounder, three six-pounders and two three-pounders, *and with three torpedo-tubes* on central fore and aft line.

The torpedo-boats should be more cheaply built, as their chief usefulness is in harbor defense and a fair percentage will be destroyed by the enemy. The torpedo-boats should be of 130 to 180 tons displacement and carry four three-pounders and two or three torpedo-tubes on central fore and aft line, according to size of the boat.

I agree with the essayist in doubting the efficacy of search-lights on " destroyers " and on larger torpedo-boats. I think that the lights would do more harm than good if used in the chase or in attempting to pick up other torpedo-boats. Search-lights on large vessels, which furnish a steady platform and which move with comparatively slow speed, do not give the desired results in clear weather over ranges of much length, and in misty weather they prove utterly worthless. Therefore, as torpedo-boats would naturally take advantage of misty and foggy weather for attacks, the " destroyer " would find its search-light a useless encumbrance, even when not considering the other drawbacks of high speed and unsteady platform.

I think that Captain Evans' suggestion, as stated in the essay, for towing a target in torpedo-boat practice, is a very excellent one, provided the target representing the cross-section of the torpedo-boat is lashed across the gunwale of one of the old condemned sailing launches or other boats that are lying in the sheds at navy yards. This would eliminate the possible collapse of the target when towing at high speed and would permit the towing torpedo-boat to use her highest speed.

When carrying out such practice attacks, why would it not be well for the towing torpedo-boat to fire a torpedo or two, when within range, at a target of suitable limits anchored just astern of the vessel to be attacked? Then, if the target in tow is not hit by a shell while passing through the same zone that the towing torpedo-boat was in when she fired her torpedoes, the torpedo-boat has been successful, provided the torpedoes she fired struck within the limits of the target fired at. If the target in tow is struck by a shell, then of course the torpedo-boat's efforts are thrown out, unless she fired an effective torpedo when at a greater range than that at which her tow was struck. This method, I think, would produce some very interesting results, as it would give the opportunity to fire torpedoes and have the section of a torpedo-boat fired upon while under conditions of actual attack. The only element wanting is that you do not surprise the attacked vessel, unless you have targets anchored both ahead and astern of the vessel to be attacked and allow the torpedo-boat to tow across bow or stern from any direction.

If the torpedo-boat gets a shot on the target before she is discovered she wins, whether her tow is struck later or not. This would give all the conditions that appertain to actual warfare.

I do not agree with the essayist in his assumption that battle-ships should be fitted with torpedo-tubes, and I also consider that torpedoes are out of place in armored cruisers and in large cruisers designed to be used as scouts. I regret that I have not the opportunity here of showing that "battle-masts" or "fighting-masts" in a battle-ship are also a menace to the fighting qualities of the ship. I cannot imagine any circumstance under which a battle-ship would dare use her torpedoes, unless it would be to give the "knock-out blow" to an already defeated and disabled enemy before he could lower his colors; and it would seem poor judgment to approach within torpedo range of an enemy that is already whipped, because *he* might possibly have an uninjured torpedo-tube and that would put both vessels upon an equal footing again, thus possibly throwing away the victory that previously had been won.

Cruisers will use their high speed to avoid engagements with battle-ships, and, therefore, battle-ships will in most cases be opposed by battle-ships or armored cruisers. In such engagements the battle-ships would probably never be within torpedo range of each other, and if by chance they should close to 800 yards, would any commander dare open his broadside torpedo ports and attach the war-head in the face of the terrific fire of his opponent's numerous rapid-fire guns?

A better target for rapid-fire guns at 800 yards than an open torpedo port in the armored side of a battle-ship could hardly be desired, and if the "men behind the guns" fail to explode the air-flask or war-head, they would most certainly destroy the tube itself. Consider the Oregon, for example. She has a bow tube, a stern tube, two starboard broadside tubes, and one port broadside tube. Her bow and stern tubes are fixed, and as they are not protected by armor, they may as well be eliminated from the discussion. The broadside training tubes are behind four inches of armor, which offers little protection against the main battery of a battle-ship. Besides, the broadside tubes could not be opened except in smooth water; the bow tube could never be used when under way excepting at very slow speed, a speed at which the Oregon's helm is of so little use that she must be handled with her engines. It is claimed from experiment that war-heads will not explode when struck by rapid-fire shell unless the small detonator itself is struck; but would any commander of a battle-ship be willing to stake the fate of his ship in battle upon this assumption, merely for the sake of obtaining a chance shot at the enemy, provided his tube and air-flask have not already been penetrated? I do not believe that any commander would so menace his own ship, when in action, as to open his torpedo-ports and attach the war-heads as long as he could fight a single gun. If every gun has been silenced and the enemy should be so indiscreet as to approach within short range, a torpedo might possibly prove successful against him; but when a ship has been so seriously battered as to have every gun disabled, it is hardly possible that her torpedo-tubes remain unin-

jured behind only four inches of armor, not to mention what would
occur when the torpedo-ports are opened and the tubes exposed to fire.
In my humble opinion, torpedoes in battle-ships, in armored cruisers
and in scouts are out of place and are a menace to the ship that carries
them, and I believe that in the near future our policy will be: *Torpedoes
in torpedo-vessels and in nothing else.*

I do not agree with Lieutenant Smith in his statement that vessels of
the Yorktown class would make " efficient scouts " if " stripped of their
heavy guns, etc." The scout must be large, with high speed, large coal
capacity and excellent sea-going qualities, because a scout's duty is to
pick up and keep in touch of the enemy in any state of weather, and then
run for the fleet. Scouts are not fighting ships; they are the information
bureau of the fleet, and their reports enable the commander-in-chief to
tell *when* and *where to strike the enemy.*

I may well quote here the splendid words of Commander Goodrich in
his discussion on page 555 of the Proceedings. Referring to the scout,
he says: " She should be large, for with increased size comes increased
steaming radius and the ability to proceed in heavy weather. She should
not have torpedoes, for her duty is to observe and report, not to fight.
Her safety lies in her speed."

Lieutenant H. O. RITTENHOUSE, U. S. Navy.—I desire to express my
appreciation of the work done by Lieutenant Smith in the study and
preparation of his subject, which is at once opportune and important in
the highest degree. He has done pioneer work in clearing for us a
confused and tangled field, a field, too, upon which, from the present
outlook, the action seems certain to depend in large measure. Further
than this, he has clearly indicated the lines of policy and construction
that it would seem wise to adopt. For my own part I find it difficult
to avoid his conclusions upon any point. At any rate, he has so
set the facts in order that debate can be kept directed to the issue, and
there can be no excuse for delay in settling upon a plan of construction.
Neither should there be delay in commencing construction. The
signs of the times are decidedly unfavorable to any further pursuit of
that wary policy of inactive watchfulness to which our legislators are so
partial. (Let us hope the country may never experience the full measure
of its economy!) We need immediately a strong fleet of torpedo-boats
to operate from and guard our harbors; and the fleet needs high-sea torpedo-boats for its defense. That systematic and business principles
directed to the sole purpose of armaments and the end of battle should
be followed in their design and construction, admits of no argument
and should need no advocate. It is difficult to conceive of a spirit in
such matters that would prefer self-interest to patriotism. These boats,
even if not directed against an enemy, would more than compensate for
their cost in the experience they would afford officers in the navigation
of our pilot waters, in cultivating sea prevision and resource, and in
developing trained crews with experience and intelligence available for
the most exceptional service.

I am heartily in accord with the essay in the moderate value assigned to the last few increments of extreme high speed when the advantages are weighed against those of other desirable qualities. The value of the last knot is about inversely proportional to the power that gains it, and a sacrifice equivalent to this power is inevitably involved.

Ensign R. H. JACKSON, U. S. Navy.—This essay, a review of the history of the development of the torpedo-boat, showing the tendency of present practice, followed by a logical deduction of the types to be used in the future, with special application to our own service, seems only open to criticism in admission of a third special type of vessel to assist the torpedo-boat as a scout. It is thought that the Desperate type, *i. e.* the destroyers, could perform this duty, assisted at times by such cruisers as might be available for scouting duty.

The selection of an enlarged Cushing or an Ericsson, with broadside tubes only, for the operations from a shore base, and a Desperate for operations with the fleet or at a distance from base, should cover the two distinct fields of torpedo-boat warfare.

A few suggestions, though not within the limits of the essay, are submitted as bearing directly upon the " Torpedo-boat Policy," viz. the minimum number of boats required of each type, the stations assigned, the *personnel* and organization.

1. Number and station: 50 Desperates and 100 Ericssons equally distributed to the following stations: (*a*) Long Island flotilla, covering coast from Boston to New York; the great commercial advantage as well as the strategical importance of a canal across Cape Cod neck would indicate that this undertaking will not be much longer deferred. This would bring Boston into the Long Island Sound district.

(*b*) Bay flotilla, New York to Florida, covering the Chesapeake and Delaware bays and interior communications.

(*c*) Gulf flotilla, from Key West to the Rio Grande.

(*d*) The Pacific flotilla, equally divided between San Francisco Bay and Puget Sound.

The boats to be assigned to the different naval stations within the district, and each boat allowed a section of a store-house in which spare parts and extra supplies are kept. The accounts to be kept at the station, and stores issued on stub orders. At present it requires almost the entire time of one officer to keep the books, make out the requisitions and returns and look after the correspondence.

The successful results attained in use of liquid fuel would point to the early adoption of it, with all the advantages of steam at short notice, smokeless combustion, rapid supply of fuel at stations, and reduction of complement of crew.

In connection with this station system too much emphasis cannot be laid upon the great gain that would result from standardizing as thoroughly as possible these boats, that suitable supplies and spare parts would always be available, and that crews may be immediately familiar with a boat when transferred from one to another.

While a boat might be sent to another station than her own, it should

only be temporarily. The whole history of the boat should belong to
one station and locality. When a boat is left with a reduced crew, her
stores and equipment would be placed in her own store-room in readiness for active service at a few hours notice.

This reduced crew to consist of a chief gunner's mate and a quarter-
master on deck, and a chief machinist and oiler in engine-room. At
no time should these men be detached from the boat. Their knowledge
and exeprience are invaluable in breaking in new crews and in getting the
best results from a boat in a short time.

With these four men on board, a new crew could be drafted to a boat
and a successful attack be achieved that night.

These billets would be eagerly sought by men from the station to
which the boat is permanently assigned.

An officer in charge of the boats of station, to take each boat out at
certain intervals to test her efficiency, drawing men from other boats and
receiving-ship for temporary duty.

On active service the officers for a destroyer to be a lieutenant, an
ensign and a past assistant engineer.

On the first-class torpedo-boats, a junior lieutenant or ensign only; a
midshipman or ensign might be added for specially arduous service or to
make up casualties.

Whereas the number of boats required is based upon the probable
demands in time of war, yet were these boats only fitted for peace service
it would be a most excellent investment, in the instruction that they
afford officers in pilotage, navigation and seamanship, with a knowledge
of the coast and harbor possessed only by a few officers on the Coast
Survey.

Above all, the responsibility of a command which the present genera-
tion knows only by tradition.

Lieutenant-Commander J. C. WILSON, U. S. Navy.—The service generally is very much indebted to Lieutenant Smith for placing before it
such a clear and comprehensive history of the development of the torpedo-boat and submitting such well-considered suggestions and opinions
as to their uses. It is a policy which I believe is less generally understood in the service than almost any other policy appertaining to the
use of naval means of attack and defense. The various kinds, sizes,
armaments and uses of torpedo-boats have changed so rapidly and multi-
plied so steadily that the average naval officer has had neither the time
nor means of keeping up with the development and the history of failures
and successes; so this essay is not only interesting, but exceedingly
valuable to enable us to bring our knowledge of the subject up to date.
I agree with the essayist as to the doubtful utility of the search-light
afloat either for attack or defense in any torpedo-boat work. In general,
I believe the importance of the search-light afloat to be overestimated.
It should be of great service on blockades, when the vessel carrying it
does not expose herself to attack by its use, and it probably would be
used to advantage in searching out positions along the coast. Its necessarily exposed position and limited range bring it within range of all

rapid-fire guns, and makes it probable that it would be "knocked out" very shortly in any engagement in which rapid-fire guns played a part. I think the essayist has shown conclusively what classes of torpedo-boats we should provide for our service, and that unless a systematic, intelligent course is pursued we will find our navy saddled with a lot of unsuitable boats. I agree with him in his deductions that but two classes (not counting the "videttes") can be properly utilized, and in any event we should first determine exactly what we want to do with our boats before building them.

It is time a settled policy of construction was entered upon and vessels constructed accordingly. The country has a right to expect that money and valuable time will not be wasted on construction of "misfit" vessels, and it would seem that the essay by Lieutenant Smith comes at a time when just such light is needed on the subject of torpedo-boat construction.

Lieutenant-Commander RICHARD WAINWRIGHT, U. S. Navy.—The Naval Institute is to be congratulated upon its Prize Essay for 1897. The publication of such an essay cannot fail to strengthen the support of the Institute, while it places before the navy a consistent torpedo-boat policy.

Lieutenant Smith first gives a concise history of the evolution of the torpedo-boat; then points out the special objects for which torpedo-boats should be designed, and, having thus outlined the qualities that have been obtained under various limitations and the qualities desired for the uses designated, proceeds to deduce logically the types that should be selected.

The essayist says: "If a board will first decide exactly to what use the boat is to be put, and what armament, speed, coal endurance and crew she will require for such use, then the displacement and horse-power will follow naturally. . . . If any other method is adopted in producing these boats, then when they are finished it will have to be determined what can be done with them." This may be said of all classes of vessels. Shall we consider to what use the vessels are to be put before designing and building them, or shall we build first and then determine what can be done with them? Shall we have a construction policy, or shall we continue to build our vessels and boats, here enhancing one quality and there another, at the expense always of some other qualities not as popular at the time, or coming under a bureau for the time being less persistent, and then turn this illogical product over to the naval officer to classify and utilize?

The question of a naval policy is a complex one, and it would not be sufficient to have a board to decide upon a type of battle-ship, another upon cruisers, and still another upon torpedo-boats. This no doubt would give us a homogeneous fleet and, therefore, a more effective one than if we adhered to the haphazard plan; but it would not prove the most effective one that could be produced for the expenditure, unless the entire question of the use of a navy to the country is considered, and the qualities required to accomplish these objects and then the types designed to develop the qualities. By this means we would settle many disputed questions and select from the numerous types the few that are needed. We would find that the principal use of the navy was to defend the coast and commerce of the country. We would define the difference between coast and harbor defense; define the limit between the mobile and immobile forces. We would settle the question between the battle-ship and the monitor. We would cease to advocate fortresses as safe refuges for our weak fleets, and cease to advocate battle-ships of light draught to enter the shoaler ports. We would remove the cloud that now obscures " the fleet in being " and would find that " a passive fleet in being " has few terrors for an active opponent; that the harbors are no place for battle-ships, and that battle-ships alone are suited to fight battle-ships in line. We would find that but a few of the harbors of our coast need defense against battle-ships; that but few need a powerful defense; that the most important points to defend are the advance naval bases; that we need a type of battle-ship to fight the battle-ships, a type of cruiser to collect information and to fight the enemy's scouts, and types of high-sea and base torpedo-boats. We might even settle the vexed question of the *raison d'être* of the armored cruiser and find that a vessel without the fighting endurance obtained from some side armor was useless for scouting purposes, and that auxiliary cruisers make the best commerce destroyers, thus erasing the unarmored cruiser type from our list.

Lieutenant Smith, in considering the general qualities, advocates strengthening the bow, even at the expense of speed, of the smaller type; and one of his conclusions that might be open to question is whether or not it might not be wise to add some protection to the high-sea type. Many torpedo-boats carry three-pounders, and while they are on a very unsteady platform, it would seem as if two or three torpedo-boats might be able to stop one destroyer if the engines and boilers were only protected by coal. This armor might be obtained by a slight sacrifice of speed or a slight increase in tonnage; the latter would entail a slight loss of speed. Whatever conclusions may be reached on minor points, the main points of the essay fixing upon two types for torpedo-boats are based on sound reasoning.

Assistant Naval Constructor R. B. DASHIELL, U. S. Navy.—Lieut. Smith's essay is most interesting, and at the present time a more important subject could not have been selected. He has clearly demonstrated the principle, what might be called the fundamental axiom of torpedo warfare, that the unprotected torpedo is a surprise weapon. With this always in view, the following conclusions seem self-evident:

(1) The torpedo-boat must be as small as possible, to obtain a degree of invisibility and immunity from discovery.

(2) She must be not only speedy, to run in quickly to torpedo range after discovery, but must have machinery capable of attaining her maximum speed instantly upon discovery.

(3) She should carry the best torpedo outfit possible, for this is her weapon, and only such guns as would enable her to overcome a vidette boat.

(4) As the chances are against her ultimate escape after attack, she should be as cheaply constructed as thorough efficiency will permit.

All these qualifications point to a small size boat. The Ericsson type seems to fulfil all requirements for such a boat, as the essayist clearly shows. But a change in her armament of guns is suggested. With nearly all our other boats, she mounts the 1-pdr., a gun which has been recently shown to be utterly powerless to stop a torpedo-boat (much less a destroyer) by injuring her vitals. This gun is therefore so much dead weight to carry about. Though possessing greater penetrative and mining power than the 1-pdr., the 3-pdr. (with ammunition) is just four times as heavy, requires more men to serve it, greater deck room, and will score fewer hits, while its recoil is so vicious in its strains upon fastenings (which must be made extra heavy to meet such strains) that all things considered, the actual value of the gun compared to the price paid for its emplacement becomes exceedingly small.

It would seem, therefore, that the machine gun is the best arm with which to check interference from vidette boats that cannot be rammed and overrun. It is light, can be mounted anywhere in a convenient socket, requires but two men, and the hits scored will be fifty to one of the single-shot gun.

Such a boat can be built for under $100,000.

Turning now to the larger type of boat, a vessel of 250 to 300 tons, the first question that presents itself is, what are the advantages possessed over the 120-ton boat? The essayist seems to select the type for the increased sea-going qualities and the ability to mount a heavy gun battery. But if the nature of our coast and the character of the defense are considered, our ports appear as the natural shelters from which the boats would make their attack. The weather must always be selected, and, as the essayist states, if the sea is too heavy for the boat to manœuvre it is unfit for torpedo work. Therefore the small boat would evidently do the work as well as the larger, her sea-going qualities being fully equal to the duty required of her.

The next consideration is the ability to carry a gun armament, presumably to destroy the enemy's boats. Her value as a destroyer depends upon the probability of torpedo-boats ever forming an important part of the hostile fleet in an attack on this country. To reach the coast there is broad water to cross, and it is not reasonable to anticipate attacks with torpedoes from any but able sea-going boats of the destroyer type, capable of accompanying the fleet at sea in all weathers. It is not wisdom to meet destroyer with destroyer; the gunboat and cruiser must be depended on to crush that type with heavy gun fire from a platform the comparative steadiness of which guarantees good gun practice. If then there be few or no torpedo-boats in the enemy's fleet, why build destroyers for the defense? Other countries are building them, but their policies, their geographical positions, are very different from ours, and their types of weapons will consequently be different. With France at convenient distance for torpedo-boat raids, England naturally builds her 98 destroyers to match the 241 French torpedo-boats. The destroyer type thus becomes a most successful and popular one, and the smaller countries of Europe and South America copy them in their orders for boats, which orders are generally placed in England. But these are not reasons why the United States should follow the same policy. What this country needs is a *large number* of torpedo-carrying craft; the value of the arm is directly proportional to the number of craft; if *five* sea-going 120-ton boats can be built for the same price as *two* 300-ton boats or destroyers, and appropriations are limited, can there be any question as to the type to be selected, both types being equally efficient for torpedo work?

The third type of vessel upon which torpedoes may be reasonably installed is the heavier cruiser or battle-ship, where the tubes are below water or protected by armor. In such vessels the torpedo is not a surprise weapon, but is used with the full knowledge of the enemy and with the ship fully exposed to counter attack against which no skill or protection can guard. Is such jeopardizing of one's ship permissible? It seems most foolhardy, most unreasonable. The art of war is to overmatch and crush an enemy by massing superior force on a weak point, *not* to match equal with equal and trust to luck for the result.

The over-water tube even behind armor is not protected, and before torpedo range is reached and after the gun contest, the fittings of port, tube, etc., will not be likely to be found in working order. Add to this the great additional weight of the torpedo installation, the cutting of large holes in the ship's side armor—armor placed there to protect her buoyancy—and the relief to the mind of the commanding officer not to have the additional complication of torpedoes to bother him, and there seems but little reason left for retaining this weapon on a vessel whose main offensive power lies in her guns. Indeed, for no other reason than the last given, the removal of torpedoes from all vessels but torpedo-boats might be advocated. The strain thrown upon hull and machinery under forced draught to obtain high results is as nothing to that imposed upon the brain of a captain going into action with all the complicated machinery in the conning tower to run, his tactics to think out, the enemy to watch. The conning tower is so crowded with steering gear, engine annunciators, torpedo directors, range finders, range indicators and similar interesting toys that the men to run them have no standing room at all.

Is there a commanding officer in the service who would not be glad to see a few of such "clock-works" removed? If there is such, he would change his mind after a few experiences of steering a course, getting under weigh, or handling the ship from the conning tower alone. So let us clear out at least the torpedo-directors, torpedo speaking-tubes, telegraph and firing keys, and give the *brains* of the ship a chance to think.

The wooden vidette launch to be carried by the bigger ships is most heartily endorsed; it is just the type of boat most needed in the service. But if a higher duty than 12 knots be required of her, she will be much lumbered up with machinery and boilers.

In naming our boats, are not the names of our venerated admirals far more suitable to a vessel of the worth and dignity of a great battle-ship, and their personal qualifications more in keeping with those of such magnificent machines, than for such dashing craft as our gallant little boats? The chief *personal* (for the boat to a sailor is a living thing) characteristics of the torpedo-boat are youth, dash, ready sacrifice. If personal names are to be employed, are there not enough Cushings, Flussers, Talbots—enough of the all-but-forgotten names of midshipmen, ensigns, lieutenants, who have given their lives for their country, to give to each boat a *young* hero's name—*pour encourager les autres?*

Wm. Laird Clowes.—It is a matter of regret to me that pressure of work prevents me from devoting to Lieutenant R. C. Smith's interesting paper the time and attention which his subject, and his manner of treating it, deserve. With the recapitulation of his conclusions as to the Torpedo-boat Policy to be pursued by such a power as the United States, I most cordially concur. At the same time I venture to think that perhaps he has not sufficiently underlined the importance of the work to be done in the naval warfare of the future by a modified Polyphemus or Katahdin; and I also venture to think that, incidentally, he gives somewhat too much importance to the ram. Of course, if only you *can* ram you are likely to inflict fatal damage upon your opponent. On the other hand, experience tends to prove, firstly, that you cannot, as a rule, ram effectively until your opponent has been rendered practically harmless and has ceased to be under control, unless indeed she be without room in which to manœuvre; and, secondly, that when you do ram effectively, you are extremely apt to do almost as much damage to yourself as to your foe.

Those are points to be carefully considered ere you set to work to build rams, with or without torpedo ejectors on board of them.

Upon the general question of the best type of torpedo-boat for war service, it is pertinent to bear in mind that although a torpedo-boat, or even a destroyer, is, relatively speaking, an inexpensive craft, and that though her expenditure in action would mean at worst no very appalling loss of life, she is, as at present built, a risky and dangerous weapon. She has her torpedoes on deck exposed to the possible rain of missiles from machine and rapid-fire guns, and should a stray shot strike an air-chamber or a torpedo's nose, the most fatal results are likely to follow.

Would it not, therefore, be worth while to add, or, rather, to prefix, to Lieutenant Smith's list of most desirable torpedo craft something like the following: Let us imagine a very handy vessel with a well-armored turtle-back like that of the Polyphemus, yet thicker, with twin screws; with only light guns; with no ram; and with a couple of submerged tubes on each broadside. A speed of 18 or 19 knots, sufficient to enable her to keep up with a fleet, would be enough. She would be almost impervious to gun fire, and she would be deadly to anything within 500 yards of her. She would use her guns only to keep off and disable other torpedo craft, and even if all her guns were put out of action, she would be offensively as formidable as ever.

I believe that this is one of the torpedo vessels, if not *the* torpedo vessel, of the future. The other types recapitulated by Lieutenant Smith appear to have their places and duties for the present, but when the new type of which I speak appears it would be practically supreme. The new

66 DISCUSSION.

type, I admit, will not be comfortable to live in unless means be adopted for submerging her only just when she is needed for action, and for enabling her, when cruising, to float high; but those means could be easily devised. Another point apparently worthy of consideration seems to me to be that the adoption of such a vessel as I describe would obviate, at least for a time, the need for making further costly and dangerous experiments with submarine boats. I am no believer that the latter will develop into efficient weapons for many years to come. In their imperfect state I grant they will possess a normal power of great value; but so also will the armored and approximately shot-proof boats which I advocate. And the latter are both cheaper to build and safer for their crews; while, moreover, there can be no question as to the possibility of making them do all that they are wanted for.

Naval Constructor Wm. J. Baxter, U. S. Navy.—The author deserves congratulation upon the able manner in which he has presented to the Institute the results of his researches and experiences. The mass of facts showing the development of the torpedo-boat has been presented in a style and with a completeness beyond question, and those who have never attempted similar researches cannot conceive the labor involved in producing results which so concisely and clearly represent the progress of naval construction in this direction.

It is to be regretted, however, that he was unable to carry his investigations further and record the results of service use upon foreign torpedo-boats of the various types. From papers, periodicals and our own Naval Intelligence reports, we know that many defects of design and detail have occurred. The defects of design are eliminating themselves as development expands along specific lines, but the defects of detail are rarely mentioned. Has not experience shown that simplicity is even more desirable and necessary in the torpedo-boat than in the battle-ship? Leaving all other considerations aside, may it not be considered an absolute necessity that on small boats where it is necessary to change the crews every three or four days, every part and fitting of armament, machinery and hull should be of such simple construction that the average seaman may learn how to efficiently operate them after a few hours instruction?

I greatly sympathize with the author's plea for some standardization of torpedo-boats, for it is precisely in the line of improvement which I have at other times endeavored to show is one of the most urgent and important questions to be solved in the near future, and some considerable experience with ships of the "new navy" has accentuated my former beliefs. The author's proposed method of having a board "decide exactly as to what use the boat is to be put" cannot be considered as his deliberate opinion, for he and all the rest of us know very well that no board can decide upon this question, as the exigencies of the service tomorrow will be entirely different from what they are to-day. A suitable board of experience and ability can decide as to the probable uses of any type of vessel during the next one or two years, but experience should also cause them to consider the probable changes which will occur during the next three or four years. Fads may be very well as a pastime, and they have done much in the development of the new navy, but the probabilities are that the fad which is the most popular the day the ship is designed, and which is the most artistically developed on a draughtsman's *chef d'œuvre*, that this fad will be most criticised, and will be the least serviceable when the ship is completed and subjected to service conditions.

Wise conservatism and intelligent simplicity are, and should be, the ruling principles with us, and I heartily concur with the author's efforts to secure them, although we may differ as to the methods.

Lieutenant PHILIP ANDREWS, U. S. Navy.—Lieutenant Smith's essay on torpedo-boats comes at a most opportune time, and is a very exhaustive technical compilation of the features of torpedo-boats and destroyers.

In view of Mr. Smith's extensive experience with the Cushing and with torpedoes, I am sorry that he did not give the Institute more of his opinions and conclusions, in addition to the large amount of data which he presents in this convenient form. I should like to hear more about the handling and tactics of the completed torpedo-boat, in groups or singly; features which interest the sea-going officer more than the development of the boats.

There is one feature to which attention should again be called: the advantage which would accrue by cutting a few more canals along our Atlantic coast. A canal across Cape Cod peninsula, for instance, would be but nine miles in length, would cost little, and would give tremendous advantage in the use of a small torpedo flotilla. It would also, if made big enough, cut off the rough and foggy trip around Cape Cod in going to Boston. There are several other points where canals should be cut, but the Cape Cod canal is instanced as probably the most important example.

This subject should be agitated through the commercial interests affected till legislation is secured. There is no more important feature of the conduct of a torpedo flotilla on our eastern coast than the most complete inland water communication.

(*Discussion continued on page 153.*)

DISCUSSION.

TORPEDO-BOAT POLICY. (*Continued from page 67.*)

Assistant Naval Constructor H. G. GILLMOR, U. S. Navy.—The author recognizes two uses of torpedo-boats. Is the same kind of boat, that is, one with the same features of speed, armament and coal capacity, best adapted to these two purposes? Is it the custom to embody in the design of coast defense vessels the same features in the same proportions that they are embodied in the cruising battle-ship? Are not the relative values of the different features in torpedo-boats which are to form a part of the coast defenses essentially different for those in torpedo-boats which are for service with the offensive arm—the cruising navy? May not the relative values of the features of a torpedo-boat of the coast defense depend upon the peculiarities of the locality in which it is intended to act?

It is to be feared that the purpose of torpedo-boats, "to destroy the enemy's ships," has, in some cases at any rate, been lost sight of, efforts being directed to the production of "the fastest boat of her size in the world" or "the fastest vessel afloat." The necessity for surprise has certainly been lost sight of in a great many cases.

It is not the intention to commence here the contention regarding the introduction of the ram, but it would seem that the proposition to make a ram of a vessel whose ratio of length to beam is ten to one and whose difficulties of local weakness are so great is ill-advised. Upon the weight allotted by the author—and it is very doubtful if it would be sufficient for the purpose—an additional 3-pounder and about a hundred rounds of ammunition could be installed, and the chances of a disabling shot from it would be considerably greater than the chances of ramming, even could that be attempted with reasonable safety to the ramming vessel.

The case cited of the Audacieux and the Chevalier should prove instructive. The angle belt of steel with a wood backing which the author speaks of was a wood chafing batten about 3 inches square, secured to the sides of the boat with two light angles, the whole being intended as a protection when lying alongside a landing or a ship. That so light a protection should have produced such disastrous results to the rammer may be taken as an index of the amount of local strengthening necessary to make ramming possible with reasonable safety.

The author has laid great strees upon the question of endurance. The method which he adopts in making comparisons of maximum power is extremely misleading and affords a very poor measure of the relative endurance of boats of different types, because of the very great variation in the maximum horse-power among them. There is usually no relation at all between full speed endurance and economical endurance in two boats unless they have exactly the same speed features. That the maximum power will only be used for short spurts and that the long distance work will be done at the economical speed is pretty well conceded.

What, then, is the justice of a comparison of a 5½ hours endurance at full speed of a thirty-knot boat with the 17 hours endurance at full speed of a twenty-six-knot boat of about the same size, when the endurance of the first at cruising speed is about one-half that of the second, instead of about one-third, as a comparison on the full-power basis would show? The column in the tables devoted to pounds per I. H. P. at the maximum power is equally misleading. The coal consumption trials of the Ardent and the Starfish, the results of which were published in *Engineering* some time ago, showed that at thirteen knots, the assumed economical speed at which the trial took place, the Ardent would steam 28½ nautical miles per ton of coal, her full capacity giving her, therefore, an endurance of 2000 nautical miles; and the Starfish would steam 39.6 nautical miles per ton of coal, so that her full capacity would give her an endurance of 2360 nautical miles. M. Normand, in his article before the Association Technique Maritime last year, gives the results of the coal consumption trials of the Forban at ten knots, her economical speed, and from these results the endurance of the Forban at ten knots would be about 2360 nautical miles. This would tend to show that in the matter of endurance size does not possess so great an advantage as might at first sight appear.

The speciousness of the author's argument in the comparison of a 22½-knot boat with a 30-knot boat will be evident by applying it successively to boats differing in speeds by successive equal amounts down to the speed of 12 knots which he assumes as the speed to be used prior to discovery. It is to be noted that this speed of 12 knots assumed by the author as the advisable speed prior to discovery is entirely arbitrary. It is obvious that the speed at which flaming at the funnels and surface disturbance begin to appear to an extent endangering the secrecy must depend upon the approach to maximum power and speed, and while it might be 12 knots in one boat, it might be 20 in another. This in itself would vitiate the comparison between the 22½-knot boat and the 30-knot boat, were it otherwise logical and consistent.

The author has made much of the maintenance of speed in a seaway. Just what are the differences between the performances of a torpedo-boat of one hundred tons and a destroyer of two hundred tons in a seaway and in still water has never been determined. It is conceivable that the conditions of sea most unfavorable to the destroyer might be very much less so to a boat of one-half its displacement and two-thirds its length; just as with ships in squadron it is sometimes found that seas most unfavorable to the larger ships have comparatively little effect upon the smaller. In any event, the difference in the performance of the two must be affected through difference in freeboard and the effect of dead weight in maintaining speed in a seaway. Then, too, there is always the question whether, in circumstances of weather seriously affecting the speed, the larger vessel would be in a postion to attack and destroy the smaller.

A careful perusal of all that precedes the author's conclusion as to "the best type of torpedo-boat" fails to bring the conviction beyond question that a boat of one hundred and fifty feet length and one hundred and twenty tons "would fill all the requirements." Even if it would fill all the requirements, is it the boat which would *best* fill all the requirements?

Should we have the same boat for both offensive and defensive purposes—the same for the defense of New York, service in the Chesapeake Bay and with the fleet? That size need not be governed by conditions of seaworthiness, within the limits of size under our consideration, has been demonstrated practically and effectively by the experiences during the past ten years of torpedo-boats varying in size from one hundred feet and forty tons upward, which have not only successfully weathered gales of great severity, but have made voyages of several thousands of miles in varieties of weather at fairly constant cruising speeds. The Batoum, the Brazilian and her two sister boats, Torpedo-boats No. 62 and No. 63 of the British Navy, boats for Japan, for China, for the Victorian Government, for India and for several of the South American States have long since exposed the baselessness of the charge of unseaworthiness on the ground of size. The possibility of seaworthiness independent of size being established, it is evident that life is no less possible to men habituated to a small torpedo-boat than to the thousands of men who yearly leave this coast and the coasts of other countries for service covering months at sea in fishing vessels whose sizes and the violence of whose motions are not greatly different from torpedo-boats, however greatly they may differ from these boats in proportions and characteristics; and that therefore this need not be taken as placing a limitation upon the size of torpedo-boats. In this connection let the remarks of Captain Eardley-Wilmot, quoted by the author on page 15, be reread. Why then "pass at once to twice the displacement at least"? Does the increase in endurance and armament necessitate this sudden doubling of displacement? Is the increase in first cost, maintenance, the number of men involved in each engagement and the loss in invisibility worth the cost?

The history of English torpedo-boat construction, from its commencement to the present (and a definite policy is not yet established) is a history of keen competition for the highest speed among a limited number of builders. There has never been a time when any type produced has been carefully and systematically tested, after training crews to the peculiar life required by the service, to determine the fitness of the type for the designed purpose, and what, if any, changes might with advantage be made. The development and its course have been determined primarily and preëminently by the rivalry of a few builders of high-speed boats, each seeking to excel the speed performance of the other, regardless of economy of power; and secondarily and partially by yearly haphazard expressions of opinion by officers high in rank, based upon a week's or at most a fortnight's observation from a distance of torpedo-boats hastily commissioned, usually with raw crews and officers new to the special service, working in one kind of weather, on one portion of the coast, under wholly arbitrary rules governing their performance. They have produced boats increasing constantly in size, displacement and speed. The end has not been reached, and speeds of 32 and 33 knots are talked of.

The "torpedo-boat destroyer" is, for the present only, the last term in the ascending series of torpedo-boats. It is the logical result of the causes which have determined the course of English torpedo-boat con-

struction. Any points of superiority—and it must be admitted that there
are some—which it possesses over the earlier members in the series,
aside from speed, are incidental to and made possible by the increase in
size which, to the English professional mind, is inseparable from increased
speed; and not the prime objects sought in the design. It is speed that
has ever been the will-o'-the-wisp luring on English torpedo-boat
builders. What has been this "several years' experience with the type"
which makes it appear "that they are just what is required for general
use with the fleet"? Each in turn has come from the builder with
column notices in the daily papers, to enjoy for a few days or a few
weeks the distinction of being the "fastest boat in the world" or "of
her class," and then be commissioned and go to serve with the fleet under
peace conditions as one of the cruising fleet, with no more effort to
determine her fitness for her definite purpose than was the case with
her many predecessors. One year it is a boat of one hundred and ninety
feet and 27 to 28 knots that is "just the thing," the next a boat of 200 or
210 feet and 30 knots, and the next a boat of 220 feet and 31 or 32 knots.
Is there any reason to believe that the end has been reached, or that five
years hence the same treatment of the subject will not demonstrate equally
conclusively that "just the thing" is a boat of 350 tons and 39 or 40
knots?

It is to be feared that the key to the author's conclusions is to be found
in this question which the author propounds in his introduction—" Which
of these different types shall we copy after for the present?"—rather than
in the incomplete reasoning which precedes them. Expressed in a few
words, the author's conclusion is that we should start in this mad race
for torpedo-boat speed about where England now is and accept their
latest type in one case, and in the other almost a duplicate of the last
thing which the English newspapers chose to call a torpedo-boat.

With regard to coal protection, all that may be said is that if the coal
is in the bunkers at the time, and the striking energy is less than sufficient
for the penetration of ¼ inch of steel and 2 feet 6 inches to 3 feet of loose
coal, the boat may be saved an occasional shot. It is, however, to be
remembered that coal is carried for use and not for protection and may,
probably will not, be there when needed and that the top coal of the
bunkers is the first used.

It would seem that the decrease in probability of complete disablement
by separation of the two engines in compartments longitudinally is considerably overestimated. It is to be remembered that in such a separation the vital target is considerably increased, for in boats like No. 6 and
No. 7, injury of the high pressure cylinder, valve chest or the steam
supply pipe of either engine would result in the disablement of both on
account of the loss of pressure through the opening so made. In the
boats designed by the Navy Department, means are provided for closing
the stop-valves of either engine from the deck, but even with this arrangement there would be an interval during which both engines would be
disabled. When we consider that the chances of such a hit being made are
practically doubled by the arrangement suggested, whatever arguments
there may be for the arrangement on the ground of increased convenience

or better distribution of weight, there can be none on the ground of increased immunity from disablement.

Lieutenant A. P. NIBLACK, U. S. Navy.—In no country in the world do the technically informed officers control the questions of types of ships and the shipbuilding policy. These are largely determined by political, financial, and commercial considerations. Nevertheless, it is of great interest to know what we ought to hope for, and no one is better qualified, in a way, than the essayist to set us straight in the matter of torpedo-boats. As an observer and in no sense technically informed, I must express my regret that in the limits of the essay so much was left unsaid which it appears to me ought to be considered under the title " Torpedo-boat Policy."

Both the navy and the shipbuilding firms in the United States have figuratively " cut their teeth " on a heterogeneous lot of steel cruisers, and at present the result is: 1st. Our new battle-ships of the Alabama class are about as nearly ideal for our purposes as human ingenuity can devise; 2nd. In the monitor type we have the highest development of inner coast line and harbor defense ships, and 3rd. When we resume building cruisers, we can, and doubtless will, so profit by the past and by results abroad as to assure the adoption of a type suited to our particular needs. It appears that in the torpedo-boat question we must also go through the teething period. Certainly the present programme is indefensible from a technical standpoint, however necessary and wise from a commercial or financial point of view.

It is a pity we cannot inaugurate at once what we, as a sensible, practical, thinking people, must ultimately come to in torpedo-boats, as we have in battle-ships and monitors (and ultimately will in cruisers), viz. torpedo-boats must suit tactics and policy, and designs must not vary at the whim of boards, designers, or contractors. The important thing is not that each ship or each torpedo-boat must be the latest thing in every detail, but that the fleet shall be homogeneous.

Effective torpedo-boat service can only be organized, carried on in time of peace and operated in time of war by boats manœuvring in company with a fixed system of tactics and with a perfect similarity in type. We have set an example to the world in common sense by limiting the speed of battle-ships to 16 knots: why not stop the equally indefensible high speed for torpedo-boats? The essayist shows conclusively its folly, but fails to drive home the real conclusion. Let us set the limit of speed for the 250 to 300-ton boats at 26 knots—good, honest, reliable *sea* speed without any question. Let us limit the first-class boats at 24 knots. This illusive and always increasing variable once fixed we may grasp the substance and not the shadow.

The true policy is to build torpedo-boats in groups either at the same time or from year to year, each group having identical tactical and manœuvring qualities, interchangeable parts, and being as nearly alike as possible.

The tests applied to the torpedo-boats of the world, which the essayist passes in review, is illusive because he fails to appreciate the wonderful system of Germany, which country has grasped the fundamental principles thoroughly. Their system is to build boats in groups, roughly, one division boat corresponding to an English "destroyer," and seven or eight first-class boats. Six torpedo-boats and one division boat form the group unit, with one or two first-class boats in reserve to keep the number up to six. The division or "mother" boat carries spare parts for the group and is practically flag-ship. All boats have single screws, and manœuvring qualities are easily obtained by a bow rudder in addition to the one astern. A flock of swallows could not manœuvre more adroitly at close distance than do the German boats.

In our country, manœuvring in groups from fixed bases, laying up in groups, scouting in groups, accompanying squadrons in groups are as clearly the real policy as for Germany. This building of individual ships and of torpedo-boats to break records and advertise particular shipbuilding firms is a great thing commercially, but not from a military standpoint. Speed costs tremendously. Four torpedo-boats that we really want, for the same money that three cost of a type we don't want, is a proposition to be commended to those who have the spending of the money. Why not use good, hard common sense and stop this folly now, instead of waiting two or three years? We don't buy race-horses for the cavalry. Of all sciences, cavalry tactics imposes definite conclusions, and so does torpedo-boat tactics, if we will only think about it.

I am not so sure that twin screws are essential, although they are a great comfort. As for strengthening the bows for ramming, I rather think that for group manœuvring the continual danger to consorts is not worth its offensive advantage in the remote chance of ramming an enemy's torpedo-boat. It would seem to me better policy to make the bow light and to give armor protection amidships at the water line, especially in view of the increased penetration and rapidity of fire of modern small arms and machine guns. Coal endurance, reliable sea speed, and seaworthiness are the benefits we may look for in reducing the speed.

I think the essayist has either somewhat lost sight of the tactical side or else does not believe in its efficiency. He is quite right in saying that the Austrian Viper does not handle well because she has only one screw; but the Natter, built by Schichau in competition with the Viper, has only one screw also, but by means of a forward rudder she handles splendidly. After all, six torpedo-boats of inferior speed and older type, but all identical, are worth more than six faster ones of heterogeneous types, unless tactics is a dream of theorists.